how to deal with:

The straying hubby on the hunt who decides that you're fair game.

The heavy-breathing boss who wants you to combine business with pleasure.

That marvelous male you'd like to mate with but definitely never marry.

Those times you want to pick up a man while making him think it's all his idea.

And last, but not least, of course, Mr. Right when he finally comes along.

A single life definitely doesn't have to be lived alone, and you can look forward to the nights when you read—

the sensuous divorcee

the sensuous divorcee

helen tumpson

A DELL BOOK

To Sidney . . .
With whom I could never have
written this book.
H. T.

Published by
Dell Publishing Co., Inc.
1 Dag Hammarskjold Plaza
New York, New York 10017

Printed in the United States of America
First printing—April 1974
Second printing—May 1974

Contents

Introduction

Single, married, and single again.

From daddy's knee to hubby's lap to upsi-daisie on your derriere.

Unless you're under thirty and know how to keep score, you're in for a shock. And unless while wedded you handled finances, plumbing, and plastering, and rubbed bellies with an extramarital buddy while still in the matrimonial manor—social changes and sudden responsibilities may send you reeling.

Maybe a playmate will wait at the gate with outstretched arms. Lucky you. If not, you're due for some unfamiliar exposure to loneliness, bewilderment, fright, plus seduction scenes that will make you wonder where the amenities went.

Get ready for reevaluation.

As a single (again) girl, you are different from the single (still) or widowed lass. The former shaped today's sexy scene. The latter has a halo: Winners in the battle of connubial bliss, they bowed only to bacteria or fate. But by their own admission and that decisive decree, divorcées are failures.

Acknowledged as toughest adversaries by male counterparts, single (still) girls can set the pace; widows are frail survivors, accorded a respectful distance for their cemeterial status; divorcées are simply considered pushovers.

The stalking male aims for all three, but with a varied approach and separate timing for each.

You, dear divorcée, are considered easy! Sudden abstinence from sexual activity is supposed to leave you wide open for love. And though your physical need differs not a whit from what other females require, most men think it does.

This book is written for the lady who wishes to love again, to take up residence with a man once more.

It advocates tongue-in-cheek serious ideas for seeking, finding, and keeping. How you can make it from misery to mastery in that brave new world you knew was there all the time.

Hopefully it will explain the hassles and how to deal with them; how the divorcée must be happily unwed before warming the cockles of a new heart, and how to calibrate those cockles to avoid another failure.

When Madame Humpty falls off the wall, only Madame can pick herself up again. Healing takes time. Survival comes from adjustment, a new frame of reference, reestablished self-esteem, and a few successful encounters in sensual situations.

For you who are overage in grade it takes more. After emerging from the legal dialectics, you will substitute new veneers for old and forget anachronistic rules for sin and sex.

Once you leaned on hubby's hand to replace bulbs and bearings, to get rid of roaches. Now you must learn to turn a wrench and crunch the bugs yourself.

Now you must develop new methods for taking off your clothes (and keeping them on). You must ignore problems that have no solution; learn to think, decide, move; pow wow on a pillow and forget.

It takes character, courage, and confidence.

But even if you are very young, very beautiful, and very rich, there are problems. And if you are middle-aged with average looks and must work to live, your road will be bumpy, most of your evenings dull.

The pandemonium in your past had to be bad, or you wouldn't have wandered. This new life will produce new hurts for a while, but will lead, hopefully, to no hurts—permanently.

So, until the initial shock and pain wear off, and the pattern of freedom becomes a way of life, don't expect to become the gay divorcée.

That comes later, luv. You must walk before you run. Try one at a time—just one foot before the other, step by step. And with this book look forward to better days with a brand new slant on survival.

Far from the Meddling Crowd

When you have cut the wifely umbilical cord, the first and best move is to move.

Those fifteen-year-old bridge-club, kaffee-klatsch, and country-club friends will blow hot and cold about your new status. Hot covers their green-eyed curiosity at the onset and outset, cold their lowered eyelids as you move off set.

When the news breaks, they gather with funereal promptness to load ammunition for lunches, dinners, teas, and whatever, which don't include you. Laden with frozen cookies from last Christmas or January's *Vogue* in April, they descend in curious packs, and while they don't ask pointed questions, they ooh and aah in pecking eagerness.

Exclaiming sympathetically about property settlement, they mentally declare you expendable and fill up that extra dinner seat with your now-available, almost ex-husband.

Ah, but you can't blame the girls. After all, they all have widowed cousins, divorced sisters. One has to look after her own. And Maggie remembers only too well how her husband chased you down the drive last New Year's Eve. So does he.

The telephone brings daily surprises, disbelief, and curiosity. The butcher, the tailor, and the corner garage dispense meat, alterations, and gas hesitantly as they weigh possible changes in your source of income.

The pro at the golf shop mumbles something about membership when you appear as usual for Tuesday's lesson. And unless you worked that out in the agreement beforehand, you just don't show up at the golf shop again.

If you had simply committed adultery, John Q. would have shut his eyes; but when you committed divorce, he shut the door. Therefore, it behooves the recent divorcée to move as far from the meddling crowd as she can go. Yesterday is not too soon. Hop in your little green coupe and drive away into the rising sun.

Go west—or any direction. But go.

After the doors close and that suddenly thinned-down ex fills all those suddenly available places at soignée dinners, more than your bladder will get galled.

Where . . . Where . . . Where

Of course the most sensible procedure is to determine where the action is.

And the action varies. A few statistics here will help you establish some sort of a ruler, but each of us has desires and needs to satisfy above and beyond the call of the wild.

Climate, accessibility, family—practical considerations come first, of course, but limit them to absolute musts, and then concentrate on the swiftest road to fantasia.

Where the Men Are

New York evidently holds the record for manpower, with more eligible bachelors than any other city. But the disadvantages of that big, cold, unsympathetic, corroded town may discourage you.

Fortitude and a partially filled purse should accompany you to the big city—the latter at least until you're safely employed.

If you want to be "where the men are" a metropolitan area is the only choice. Although New York does have more of everything, including fog, smog, dirt, smells, mugging, and drugging, most of the other major cities are not much better. You'll just have to put up with a little pollution if you want to zero in on the available nailables. And for those of you who wish to be scientific in selecting a new abode, here behold the figures for single men in major cities of the United States according to population:

CITY	NO.	POPULATION	SINGLE MEN	PERCENTAGE OF POPULATION
New York	1	7,895,563	881,171	11
Chicago	2	3,369,359	375,514	11
Los Angeles	3	2,816,061	318,375	11
Philadelphia	4	1,950,098	215,563	11
Detroit	5	1,512,893	161,761	13
Houston	6	1,232,802	113,325	9
Baltimore	7	905,759	97,609	10.7
Dallas	8	844,401	72,452	8.5
Washington	9	756,510	99,908	13
Cleveland	10	750,879	77,947	10.3
Indianapolis	11	745,739	64,035	8.5
Milwaukee	12	717,372	76,978	10.7
San Francisco	13	715,674	105,251	14.5
San Diego	14	696,769	100,798	14.6
Boston	15	641,071	92,762	14.4

Geographically there seems to be a reasonable choice, and even weatherwise a variety is evident. If you have the time and where-with-all, take a flying tour. A brief test of new territory isn't very satisfactory, but a little is better than none. If an immediate decision is mandatory, fall back on the atlas or your traveled friends. Or shut your eyes and point. Let luck and the fickle finger of fate direct your new destiny. They probably will anyway.

Unless you've tons of that long green, don't resort to resorts. The competition from the "haves" is just too stiff for the "haven't quite enoughs." In most sandy, sunny regions women outnumber the men. In addition to slim pickin's, the pickin's are smug and spoiled. Even vacations are better spent away from paradise islands. Try Alaska or Australia, where men outnumber women fifteen to one.

If you're still responsible for little ones, that makes a difference too. In fact, maybe you had better stay home and read another book. It's really better to board that motorcycle single-o than to navigate new terrain with under-twelves riding shotgun. Kids don't cotton much to change, and diaper service just isn't the same in motels.

Another tip for travelers—avoid new towns with old relations. Even close ones get distant when needled by inner guilt. Their responsibility to play protector is nonexistent, and once the token coins are thrown in the toll box they disembark. Count on brothers, sisters, aunts, uncles, cousins, and godfathers for nothing. Anything more than that is bonus and very, very rare.

Try not to move in with Mama either. Unless finances or health preclude independent action, slipping into the premarital state with parents dooms hopeful dames to Shrivelsville.

Mom assumes old protective attitudes and pontificates with unsought, outmoded advice. Worst of all, she waits up till her thirty-two-year-old baby comes home, and wrapped in rollers and blue flannel robe, flings open the door when she hears your key. Her histrionics are Academy Award caliber. "Thank God, you're home! I was so worried." If you think that greeting surprises baby, you ought to see the expression on the face of her date!

Daddies aren't so bad. They long ago ceased to weep over your lost virginity and returned to the newspaper. But anyway, bypass the old homestead and opt for a *very small* apartment.

Shucking the Corn

Breaking up is "oh so sad, oh, oh, oh." That old tune belongs rightly to the task of packing up a shattered household. When the shards of yesterday's happiness fall out of the dresser drawer, it's difficult not to lapse into gloom. Rid yourself of all reminders of a once-happy life. Buy a *very large* waste can. Place it in the middle of the room. Fling like a discus thrower and don't look back.

Like Lot's wife, hindsight will only avail you salty tears.

Indecision should mean a no-no. You will regret surplus far more than doing without. Along with old wedding dresses, dump sentiment. You are entering a new era of memory-making, so pile that basket high, and don't hold onto your (old) hat.

For the tax conscious, don't forget that any con-

tributions of household articles or clothing to recognized nonprofit organizations are deductible. See
your accountant for details.

A tough and tiring job, but one that ends, finally. So that one fine day you wake with the
closets empty, furniture sold, bags packed, and the
future on your doorstep. One last cup of coffee
and off you go.

Oh yes, a reminder, don't forget to stop the paper.

And once again, don't look back.

New Horizons

Driving into a new skyline pumps up the old adrenalin.

Especially if you arrive in an untried town hungry, tired, and late. No red and gold neon can brighten night cities enough to make them familiar when they're not. And when this already lonesome Georgia checked into that first motel she felt illicit, unfunded, and followed.

Furtive glances and trembling hands were just old stuff to the room clerk, however. He remained brisk, courteous, and cool while she signed and feverishly snatched up the key. "Just moving to town?" he offered.

"Why, yes, how did you know?"

"Spot 'em every time," he smirked with a bottom-toothed smile.

But that's just in the beginning. The old nerves

steady up after a while, and pretty soon there's no one you can't stare down.

Be patient. Be brave.

And look for an apartment—and a job.

The Apartment

If you choose to hold old lines and fly your flag in home territory, you can skip this chapter. Each man to his own poison, and each woman to her favorite folly. But to the easily offended: gird your tear ducts and extra blinkers to become an expert in the eyeball-to-eyeball confrontation. Financial security helps too. If you are in the 400 (thousand) strata no doubt you will still be clinking glasses at all the ho-hum social events. But since most of us lack that kind of economic solidity, you will only hear that clink in the sink after the big divorce.

For you who hurry off to seek your fortune in distant cities, orchids. Before you raise the sails, however, do yourself a favor. Get up one morning early, before dawn, when the horizon is very, very dark.

No stars, no moon.

Suddenly the sun pours rose and gold into the sky, brilliantly waking pastelled rooftops.

It could happen to you.

In taking off for parts unknown, be prepared for that darkest darkness before dawn. And then, baby, throw your arms around the dazzling new day— yours, all yours.

The new city will seem unfriendly, at first. Even a map won't help a lost lady every now and then, so take your time. Call a distant cousin who knows Newtown's suburbs and city divisions and who lives where and why. Or drop in on the local chamber of commerce and chat with the director. Usually one of the area's most personable citizens, he will brief you with glowing terms about his city. And maybe, if *you* glow a little, he'll spring for a Coke.

(Always be alert for any kind of possibility— job, man, whatever—you just never know.)

Visit the AAA for maps, city history, industrial information, travel tips. Find out where the new apartment complexes are mushrooming. Swish in-to a singles building between five and seven o'clock and dig the daddies as they swing on home. And always check the parking lot. Nothing else is a better barometer of what's upstairs than the kinds of cars waiting below. Caddies and Volvos, Oldsmobiles and Renaults are a lovely indication. But beware, the rent probably matches the chrome!

Stay away from retreats of the retired. No matter how cheerful the lobby, that hall silence is deadly. A posh apartment is definitely a plus but not in the environment of the aged. You, in the best years of your life, ought to be where the action is.

Of course, you will try to get the most for your money, and a location that ultimately suits your job area choice. But most important in the selection of a home is to determine if you are WDD (Within Dating Distance) and GA (Geographically Acceptable). Guys today aren't even willing to meet you halfway if three expressways and a toll road separate your dwellings.

This categorical problem is a kind of puzzle. You really have to guess. But there are a few guidelines: single men usually select apartments near their offices and town clubs, or hang their hats near their golf bags or tennis rackets.

Check out the popular country, golf, tennis, and boat clubs and their attendant high-rises or town house complexes.

Don't be afraid to walk into the manager's office anywhere to ask for prices, admittance policies, dues, accommodations, part-time privileges, etc.

And once again, keep your baby blues wide for accidental eyeballing at every corner in the club.

Have a Coke in the bar, or lunch in the coffee shop on visiting days. A great place to note your possible neighbors.

If your pre-permanent pad and ante-job finances permit, take your time. If not, even an immediate decision requires careful evaluation of the questions posed.

But, really, anyway it happens, there's a lot of luck involved. Don't sweat it, though, and don't wrinkle that creamed brow. Sign a year's lease only. It will take you that long to get acclimated, and then you can always move. If the owners are willing, by all means take a monthly lease with option to sign on for a year or longer at the same rent. Unfortunately, not many landlords are willing.

If you favor a furnished apartment, be sure the lease notes all scars, burns, scratches, and missing table leaves. Check the house carpet for spots, streaks, worn areas. If you bring your own, be sure to ask permission to hang mirrors, pictures, bookshelves, and write that into the lease, too. The friendly rental agent won't be nearly as friendly when you depart. And his sticky fingers will be loath to return your one-month rent deposit for security. *Put all problems in writing,* before they can be attributed to you.

With reference to living alone, one last word of caution. CAUTION! That means TAKE CARE! City streets are no longer safe to walk at night, and single females are often the prey of muggers and prowlers, even in their apartments.

A high-rise with a doorman and/or a night watchman makes for relaxed sleeping. To protect your beddy-bye dreams, have a dead lock, a night latch, and a peep hole. *Never* open the door to someone you don't know, and memorize the telephone number of the police station nearest you. Precaution makes *you* the most dependable person that you can depend on.

Now, you've gotten a pretty good look at your new home town and you've lucked into living quarters with a divine view from a romantic terrace and—

Well, before we get into the nitty gritty of this maneuvering, we'd better get you a job. And for more reason than just earning even necessary money—for your peace of mind.

The World of the Formerly Employed

To be sure it's pleasant, every once in a whirl-wind, to enter a period of inactivity. To have nothing to do. To loll with glass and magazine on the sofa, or sun near the surf, or window shop with no timetable. But not often. And certainly, positively, absolutely not when a traumatic experience (death, taxes, divorce) is exacting its pound of flesh from the psyche.

Even if you are diamond-embossed and gilded, you will touch bottom in moments of despair and disparagement after the judge declares you free. Self-abasement can become a full-time occupation. Work is the only medicine that soothes the deep wound of loneliness.

Hard work.

Away from home.

Let's just assume you can use the money. Volunteer efforts at this time don't provide the pride of accomplishment that you will need. So, after the furniture is polished and the lamps placed and the family portraits stuffed into the junk trunk, start to read the paper. The classified section.

The first reading will provoke bewilderment. Advertisements for help are there in profusion, but what kinds of jobs are these? Relax. Although most of the offerings are not your cup of tea, you could, you *really* could fill most of the requirements for *most* of the ads. And usually, big jobs start with little ones.

That means you have some ability . . . you do have a base to start on, and all you need is guidance. Do you type? Are you out of practice? Call the IBM people, rent an electric typewriter, and practice for a week. Typing can get you into the environment you want; talent and personality can move you into the position you like. Good office help is always at a premium, and if you have stenographic abilities you need never be without employment.

But how to get situated when your skills are almost past renovation and your talent (former) not office material anymore?

Just close your eyes and jump.

Call an employment agency. Call several and make appointments. Be immaculate. Try the impeccable put-on. Smile. State your abilities. Be positive. If you sound confident, you will convince yourself as well as the interviewer.

Put together a résumé. If you've forgotten how,

visit the public library where you can study the various forms. As you combine the bits and pieces of your background, don't be surprised to see a larger picture emerge than you remember.

Let's see, you worked for that ad agency for two years after you were married. And when Clarice was three you·ran a nursery school for a year so she could attend. And later on you put together three, no four shows for the Junior Women's Club . . . script, scenery, all of it. And didn't you write Uncle Harry's advertising for a year or so when he couldn't afford professional fees?

And listen, baby, you can fudge a little. That gray area gets a lot of overtime action; looks good on the top of the pile; rarely gets checked out. Just don't say you can do something that you can't. Dazzled with the footwork, your enchanted employers might just want a demonstration of talent.

Where to look for employment? Where are the most jobs open for the highest wages to women? Alas, there appear to be no figures available to answer this question. Even the Bureau of Labor Statistics has no very good measurement of areas that offer the best working opportunities to females.

The national average of working women in metropolitan areas is 37.8 percent. Further digging in the Labor Department's Women's Bureau indicates that there are six areas that have a greater proportion of women in their total workforce than this national average:

Washington	41%
San Francisco	40%

Oakland	40%
Baltimore	39%
Chicago	38%
St. Louis	38%
Houston	38%

These cities have a high proportion of governmental, clerical, insurance, financial, and white-collar opportunities. Generally, the industrial cities like Cleveland or Detroit have a greater number of blue-collar jobs, and tend to have a low percentage of women in positions held.

The Women's Bureau keeps these statistics only for the top twenty metropolitan areas, but it suggests the possibility that women may find even wider opportunities in smaller cities, or in certain sections of large cities with a high proportion of white-collar jobs. State capitals, for example, or midtown Manhattan.

These figures represent only *past* opportunities, relative to men. The Labor Department has not figured the unemployment rate for women in each of the cities, so there could very well be a great number of jobless there, as well as a lot of jobholders. To repeat, there is just no measure of the number of job vacancies open to women only, which is the figure needed to gauge what opportunities exist. Perhaps soon, with the strengthening position of Women's Lib and its advocates, further studies will be made in this area. Such material would be helpful not only in determining employment availability, but in deciding a career.

Since there is no way to determine the most secure city jobwise, you might as well concentrate on the manpower statistics and go from there.

Take your classified clippings, agency leads, and all the gumption you can summon. Of course you want equal pay for equal work, but your smile, good looks, and charm are the best weapons to achieve position and the salary you deserve.

Remember, no one ever got a job by explaining what they couldn't do. If you have a tune, play it. Loud and clear. Forget "I forget" and don't say "I don't."

Be charming and direct. Don't flirt. Do smile. Don't cross your legs. Don't wear a mini skirt to interviews. Don't wear pants or pants suits. Don't pick your cuticle or file your nails. Don't smoke. Don't accept a drink. Don't become familiar playing "do you know's" from his home town or yours.

If the interviewer needs someone to fill an immediate opening, and if you are willing and determined, personable and polite, chances are they'll take a chance.

Then it's up to you.

Keep in mind that sooner or later you will find a niche that fits or almost fits. Even the search sharpens your wits.

Employers today appreciate the woman returning to work. If she's childless or past the child-bearing stage, she's more likely to become closely involved with the business at hand. And just as important, she is less likely to switch jobs than a younger, less responsible miss or ms.

My (Your) Blue Heaven

Ah, the pity of it all! You've got a new job, in a strange city, and an unfamiliar apartment. What's worse, you've contracted a virgin (for you) disease—loneliness.

When you turn those two keys into that fortressed pad, it begins. Lump in the throat or pain in the belly. Tears. And only the sound of your own sobs as you lean over the balcony or press your brow against the windowpane.

And maybe, to complete this masochistic scene, you light a candle or two, so that when darkness falls, only your shadow flickers on the bare white walls.

Go ahead, feel sorry for yourself.

Everyone does.

One of the cheapest and most effective sources of solace is self-compassion. Coursing down puffing cheeks, warm tears are soothing, if salty. A necessary safety valve, providing they don't replace the olives in a martini.

At this juncture, the inner you scrapes bottom. A nagging doubt begins that even a bad husband would be better than no husband. And a sharp-nosed virago predicts future failure to add to your wasted past.

Cry—but—

Cry alone, and not in your beer. Despair, beat your yearning breasts, but don't uncork the bottle.

The first trials will end, and the second begin. Time now to remember that darkness before dawn, with its attendant flash of dazzling gold.

Important! Don't drink alone. Ever.

If you feel you must have a drink, call an office pal and down a highball together. Then go out for dinner and bemoan your destiny together. I promise you, unless your legs are bowed and your hair green with fuzzy purple patches and your tummy in tiers, there's a better day and a man comin' your way.

Yes, the worst hour in the first six months of divorce is coming home alone, knowing there's no one to hear the key in the lock.

But this, too, will pass. And you will make it . . . like all your separated sisters, to new friends and a fondness for occasional solitude in your blue haven.

The Mating Gain

Meeting men requires finesse. After all, the wary male practices his avocation daily, so you must also. While he is making wary, you must be sure he is making Mary.

It's not as difficult as the girls say. Or maybe they just don't have the knack; or maybe they haven't concentrated on developing a technique.

But *you* don't have to fret, my pet.

Let me take you by the hand while we wander through the masculine mind, down masculine byways to masculine haunts . . . Then will we make our way to a cul-de-sac, meeting place *extraordinaire* . . .

Misconceptions abound in the advance of male to female and vice versa. Loneliness and the inability to make contact are not restricted to the feminine gender. It isn't really unusual to buzz

Mr. Hotpants on Saturday night and find him at home in bed, alone. Some men are just as choosy as you are.

Moreover, dear heart, many men (especially divorced and widowed ones) are shy. Like you, they've been out of circulation; and the old games of flirting, dating, and moving-in are new and uncomfortable. Their fear of being refused equals your desire to be asked, and rejection only adds to their reluctance to make that first approach.

So, you must discard outworn standards for current practice. Really, most of the time it will be up to you to initiate the action. But there's a trick to kindling this kind of a candle.

He mustn't know.

Masculine vanity requires that he make the advances. Even Herbert Horney will turn away from the obvious female predator who bares her slippery fangs.

That's it.

Be Zsa Zsa Gabor in a Doris Day smile. Be Boris Karloff with a Bing Crosby lilt. Too tough? Ridiculous. Just the same old feminine wiles that got you the new kitchen from reluctant hubby way before the bust; or was it a mink coat, baby Jane?

Same deal.

Out of the Ordinary Places to Meet

1.

Setting: Tip-Top Restaurant, across from the
          office.
Time: Noon
Characters: 1. Strange man
             2. Andrea

Enter Andrea, beautifully attired in correct office garb: tailored dress just above the knee, light lipstick, twinkling, roving baby blues. She zeroes in on an empty counter seat next to a DHM (Dark Handsome Man), who is carefully reading the menu.

HE *(laying aside menu):* Waitress, I'll have the mackerel with two vegetables . . . that low-cal lunch.

ANDREA *(picking up menu):* Ummmm, oh, dear.
  (Pause . . .)

ANDREA: Oh, my.

HE: What's the trouble?

ANDREA: I never can decide what to eat. Gosh.

HE: That mackerel is always delicious. Low calorie,
  lots of vitamins, why don't you try that?

ANDREA: Okay. That sounds marvelous. Waitress,
  I'll have the mackerel, too.

There! See what Andrea has in common with
the stranger? Mackerel. Strange entree . . . but
wait until the main course. Andrea's new friend
picked up her check, walked her around the block,
turned out to be a prominent lawyer . . . unmarried to boot. Now they are holding hands in intimate little bistros, and I hear they have switched
to lobster.

2.

Example again. Helpless Jackie took her weekly
wash into the neighborhood laundromat. She
fluffed soiled silks in with no-iron sheets and retired to the side lines with (surprise) *Sports Illustrated.* Starting at the beginning she concentrated on a delicious feature about football in the
sixties. One eye, however, watched the fourth machine to the rear and its careful user—blond, be-
spectacled, and unsure. Once his machine was
underway he selected a waiting chair only one re-

moved from Jackie. She popped both eyes furiously back into *Sports* and waited. Then: "Excuse me, sir, but would you mind explaining a double reverse to me? In football, I mean."

He was delighted. With a pencil stub, on the back of somebody's forgotten pillowcase, he mapped out football plays in double reverse until Jackie almost understood. A feat, indeed, since she didn't really dig football. She had simply watched this gorgeous male play touch tackle with high school lads in a nearby park. And once she saw him carrying a small bundle of shirts into this very laundromat. It wasn't until four months, thirty dates, and three football games later that he found out she had a washer and dryer two doors down the hall. When he asked her one evening if she had any back issues of *Sports Illustrated,* he was confused indeed. She answered, *"Sports Illustrated?* What's that?"

Well, we've touched on lunch counters and laundromats. Now where?

Everywhere.

Earlier in this guide I suggested that you stay peeled for possibilities all the time. That's the key.

3.

What if you spot a handsome hungry male in the supermarket? After two or three cart encounters you feel almost certain he is unattached. No wedding ring, small amounts of fruits, vegetables, and steady purchases of strip steaks . . . the best. He is neat, clean, tall enough, wears sneakers and jeans. And he smiled at you. Twice.

This, lady, is not the time to buggy off! Outflank, surround, and strike!

Use binoculars if you must, but mark his moves at least two aisles away. Check his speed. Determine his direction. How up, how down. And meet him, coming round the bend, uh, head on! Don't nod. Don't smile.

Be prepared with a jar of kosher pickles and drop them on contact! Your embarrassment will arouse his protective instincts (as long as you don't splash him with pickle juice. Make it an easy drop, okay?). Anyway, blush, stammer, and look helpless. It's not a bad idea to kind of splatter your pretty pants with dilly drops. Concern will pave the way for openers, and you can continue perusing in his direction.

When the introductory remarks are concluded and a rendezvous arranged, be sure to go home and change clothes. Pickle juice hasn't the aroma of love.

4.

Have you ever had an interest in stocks—buying and selling? Ticker tapes are fun and brokerage houses exciting. Karen T. lost a happy ten pounds by spending her lunch hour at Merrill Lynch, Pierce, Fenner & Smith.

Her interest was more than financial. One of

the brokers got stuck on an elevator with her. The mechanical equipment was only disabled for ten minutes, but Mr. Broker was disarmed for life.

Karen noticed the initials MDFS on his handsome leather brief case during the elevator incident. Immediately the little lady was overcome with an unquenchable desire for a portfolio of her own. She learned to read the board from the "elevator" man, achieved a more than negligible profit, and walked off a twin winner—with both man and money.

5.

Sports offer a spectacular opportunity to see what it's all about. If you like the snowy reaches try skiing. And even if glissades make you shiver just to think about them, how about just acquiring a dazzling ski suit and a fireside manner. Most of the winter mating game is played indoors anyway, although it's nice to have those snow-scrubbed cheeks. But if you do ski, and if you're very lucky, the lift will stall exactly when you're riding high beside glamorous Gregory—handsome, strong, and very warm. If you planned it that way, Zsa Zsa, don't forget about Doris!

6.

If you're a Southern belle, and boats are your passion, visit a shipyard. Believe it or not, lots of intrepid millionaires buy sixty-foot yachts. Lots. All you have to do is find one.

I personally followed this avenue, and though I didn't meet a buyer, I met a seller—a charming, British salesman of yachts. Nothing like the life of a lady sailor for exploring uncharted seas.

Another happy hunting ground for boatmen is the yacht club . . .

Usually private, they require real or forged invitations to come aboard. A little practice should precede this test of ingenuity, but there are ways.

Arrive in tennis shorts and ask at the desk for a fictitious friend. When advised that your racket is the wrong gear for this shore, burst into tears. If there is a lolling yachtsman about, and your legs are fetching enough, he is sure to try to change your sport.

Apply for membership. Request a tour of the premises and hope for that eyeball contact mentioned earlier. Don't leave without checking the bar, or having a cup of coffee in the snack shop.

7.

If you love airplanes, visit the local airfields, the small ones. This is practically virgin territory for lonely gals who dig flying. When your salary starts an upward flight you might even board a trainer to find new horizons with wings. And whoever heard of anything but a dashing pilot!

In these environs you should display great

amounts of self-sufficiency. Sportsmen like women who can keep up, who won't blubber in a squall, or panic in a forced landing. If you are a copilot person, you are very special indeed. Boat women, sky women, are hard to find for boatmen and skymen. My informants talk wistfully of a legendary female who can drop the mainsail in thirty-mile gusts, or fly smiling under thunder and lightning through an unavoidable storm. Josephine, if you're fearless, you're beautiful.

Do you think these male pursuits too far afield for your first efforts? Maybe so, but keep in mind that the common orbits of the single male are crowded with eager adversaries.

8. Crossing the Bar

When cocktail hour strikes, between five and six, the neighborhood saloons fill up with searchers of both sexes, and if you're an amateur you haven't much chance. Even getting a drink at a crowded bar is a sweaty proposition, with body contact like bargain day at Macy's.

But if you insist on having a go at the swinging pubs, once again you ought to follow the form.

Monday nights are dead. Only traveling salesmen are available on Mondays; Tuesday nights the crowd improves, but not much.

Try the noon group for early in the week. Somewhere in the vicinity of your office there has to be a pub-restaurant where you can dine at the bar, and where camaraderie increases as the weekend nears. These taverns are really fun, but beware of "everydayism." Not more than once a week in any saloon and better once a month.

Thursday evenings are more lively than MTW, but really, girls, only the uninitiated haven't heard that Friday is trolling night. Mating aims are overt, and every bistro vibrates with contact activity. Hands, eyes, and address books move rapidly in the darkened cabarets; love, or something, marches on.

9. Office Love—Can It Last?

When two people meet at the water cooler for a quick kiss or send secret notes through the in-out box, it isn't long before the whole office knows. There is a marked drop in office output as staff measures amorous input. Everybody loves a scandal, no matter how slight. What the boss doesn't know he will soon find out, and you may be holding hands on the sidewalk after a couple of mooney coffee breaks.

If you have to encourage a magnificent co-worker who finds you absolutely irresistible, haul out your high school acting trophy and pretend you don't know him from nine to five.

The evenings will be more exciting anyway when you finally meet (secretly), at your apartment.

Hug and kiss and make fun of the deceived, but play it cool on corporate terrain.

10. You'd Never Expect . . .

Bonus areas for bumping into someone special really abound.

One girl I know met her present husband in the library. Both of them love to read and now spend every weekend filling bookshelves together.

11.

Flea markets fascinate collectors, and every city has Sunday bargain wares displayed for ardent rummagers. While you're eyeing antiques, don't overlook the male antiquers. And if a fascinated collector admires your grandmother's brooch, don't fail to capitalize on your cleavage. If you haven't much of that, fall back on Shalimar; perfume often makes a man forget just what he was looking for in the first place.

12.

Stoplights are challenging grounds for sophisticated rogues. Eye contact, a smile, and tacit agreement can all occur within sixty seconds. Try it, afternoons only, and don't be surprised to see that interested eye in your rearview mirror when the light changes to green.

Caution here. Don't let him follow you home.

Go to the drug store or supermarket, where you can both climb out and say hi. If he looks as good away from the wheel, check his cards, credentials, etc.

Don't be hesitant about asking who, where, what. No rational man expects a reasonable lady to succumb instantly to a strange male. On today's fast track most faces are unfamiliar. Normal or perverted? Your experience and intuition are usually dependable barometers.

If you have any doubts, sneeze, blow your nose, and cough. Your near pneumonic attack will excuse a fast dash for the Contac counter.

By now, you've got the idea.

Recognize that routine is the fabric of life, and that is where you can best meet your man—in the daily exercise of *his* routine.

13.

Everybody goes to the bank, and sooner or later you will notice familiar faces filling out deposit slips when you do. If you like one of the faces, "lose" a dollar and let him pick it up.

"Did I drop that? Oh, how can I ever thank you?"

Well, if you're going to get that excited, maybe you'd better chance it with a fiver. Always keep the props commensurate with the ruse.

14.

Most men patronize a single filling station. You ought to also. And if you buy enough gasoline, you'll soon spot those regular customers. If you can swing it, manage to have your tanks filled simultaneously and compliment his car. If he admires yours, and you, and offers to fill your tummy-tank, go, girl, go.

15.

If you like bridge and are a genuine devotee, search out the duplicate bridge clubs. Men who play this game seriously adore women who can recount hands and know when to go for slam.

Refrain from idle chitchat, bid firmly, and play efficiently.

After you've co-captained a few winners with your quarry, forget to bring your car. Elated, he will take you out for coffee, propose a tournament tie-up, and notice that your eyes are a deep, warm brown.

That's the way it happens.

16.

Improve your mind. It can't hurt, and it might lead to expansion of your social life. Evening

schools are a way of life. You could fill your schedule with available classes, some free, some involv-
ing a slight fee at local education centers and col-
leges. Just to avoid crowds (of other women) try
a course in finance or international protocol. Find
fields that draw established executives, and if you
haven't the prerequisites, ask if you can audit. If
none of the learners or the lecturer have any appeal, you can always stop listening. But maybe
you can gather in a passing grade and more than
a passing fancy.

Now you're beginning to think creatively. You,
as a desirable liberated woman, can make life happen for yourself. You can create excitement and
fun by thinking positively. And you can meet all
the men you want by just being where they are.

17.

Friends sometimes come through. Not often, because married people don't usually pal around
with the unattached. But occasionally a newly
widowed male is taken in tow by sympathetic buddies, or a recently divorced gentleman is invited
to dinner. You get to f.ll in, regretfully most of the
time. But once in a while the dandy dish is delicious, and you come up with a king.

18.

Church affiliations are rarely fruitful, but there again, if you're so inclined it can't hurt to try. Maybe sweet gentle disoriented Sidney will share your prayer book and ultimately altar your life. This reverent source also deserves at least a visit to the pew.

Remember the credo of the crafty—leave no stud unturned!

19. Are There Any Ocean Worthies?

If you adjust well to ups and downs . . . try a weekend for singles at sea.

Maybe you won't bag a kingfish (marriage material), but you might catch a channel bass (company for the cruise). No man is no loss, however, since salt air is a cure-all for aches and pains, blues and blahs, muscles and skin.

Barring hurricanes or waterspouts, you ought to have a ball.

Tally read about a singles cruise in Sunday's paper. Special sailings for the unattached featured gambling and gamboling in nautical luxury. The ship she chose made short runs in the Caribbean and offered middle-class fun for medium fares. Some made whoopee all night on deck, without a bed to rest their head. Others paid more for bunk and bath, two to four in a room. You could bring your own (same sex) or be assigned a buddy (same sex) by the reservations clerk.

A two-day trip with meals and entertainment was under sixty per person, with top fares twice that figure for the very fanciest deck.

Tally took a $69er and a shipmate, who paid the same. Their quarters were midships with shower, toilet, and almost enough room to dress simultaneously, nose to nose and toes to toes.

It was Halloween. Poking through clouds, an almost full moon spangled deck spooners with lazy light. Tally was underwhelmed with the choice of singolos—and wary, but moonbeams bewitch even the wary. Bored, poor Tally got hung up on the cook. Happily her bass was chatty and charming and danced tremendously well.

Her friend was lucky, too. She met a kingfish, looking for a partner. Of course, she was keen on being courted, and their romance headed out to deeper water.

Cruise ships are designed to make people happy. You can always go home, with tall tales, even if only about creature comforts or OPP (Other People Pair-ups). Shipboard alignments are faster on a weekend jaunt, and among a small percentage action is almost immediate. An estimated ten percent are certain to end up in the sea sack. Some of the more ambitious acquire more than a first mate, making quick belt notches in a frenzied dash from doll to doll or guy to guy. Others, helpless in the frantic mixing, languish alone in the darkened lounge.

Class of clientele on bargain rate cruises varies. Tally met truck drivers and salesmen, a retired captain, and a shy but scholarly mailman.

Cardinal rule for single ladies at sea: don't be trapped in the troll. If a quick chat with Harry leaves you cold, leave him. Try another. If a fella fails to grab your tab for a Scotch, leave him. Try another. Remember though—as in other single gatherings—there are usually more gals than guys.

Most of all, avoid the sea-single Casanovas. They shed their wedding rings for the shipboard action, but return to the family hearth immediately in port.

These married singles are obvious. They laugh more, wink, seldom relax. Hoping to find a quick, though temporary heaven, they come on like Fuller Brush men. Avoid these dingdongs. Their samples are a waste of spray, and they come without a guarantee.

But, if you have the opportunity, time, and a good supply of Dramamine . . . by all means embark. Boats are synonymous with adventure, luxury, and romance.

Who knows, little mouse, you might lasso a lion at sea.

Les Misérables — Married Men

What is available without any effort on your part, and available in any size, any weight, any afternoon, is the married man.

He thinks you need him. And he knows he needs you.

From about age thirty-nine on, the American male feels suddenly threatened by imminent loss —of youth, ambition, hair, future, and virility. He broods himself into a lather of frustration, compounded by real and imagined signs of deterioration. He is tired of his job, his wife, and his responsibilities. There seems, suddenly, only one more chance before he is inevitably caught in quicksand.

He thinks about chucking it all. Running away to a desert island, or better still, one inhabited only by beautiful Polynesian maidens.

Some do. Each year, in this country, an undetermined but enormous number of married men are reported missing. It's doubtful that they find those exotic gals or end up owning a banana plantation. But most malingering males just sigh and keep carrying their briefcases back and forth on the New Haven or Long Island Railroad.

Some of them use booze; some turn to the track. Some of them are just waiting for you.

If you are reasonably attractive, recently divorced, and you gravitate into their territory—watch out for that insidious first assault.

They know you are lonely and accustomed to masculine company. Also accustomed to something else, in almost daily doses, for which you no longer have a source!

The infiltration begins with cocktails. Sometimes the gung-ho Lothario fires up with lunch. The excuse for either can be any trumped up trivia—mutual friends, a new job (with more dough, of course), or just a "you really ought to see this fantastic restaurant and I'll take you" line.

Bah-lone-ee!

Except that if he is good-looking and fun (most married men are—they're so carefree), you will probably be enchanted, intrigued, and sucked in. After you've taken the bait, it's easy (for him).

He plys you with martinis, holds your hand to gypsy violins, and tells heart-rending stories of a sterile home life. His wife neither understands him nor appreciates his exceptional achievements.

After a steak dinner and proper vintage Beaujolais, he confesses more, wishing that his wife were like you. But *not* that you were his wife.

He uses that most effective line more than once.

"You need me and I need you! Oh, how I need you!"

If he has any money he lays it on the line.

If his finances are shaky he implores you to see him occasionally just for *l'amour—toujours l'amour.*

After divorce, you could encounter invitations to illicit suppers every day. In fact, an unending line of still-spliced Casanovas will hover at your gates of freedom.

Yes, I accepted a few summonses to dine. Prime beef makes me sympathetic. Afterwards, if the confessions got sticky I could go home. And usually did, with full tummy and clear conscience.

But it's not always that easy.

When violins are soft and melodic, and the hand on yours warm and comforting—and when you're lonely—even the best laid plans . . .

An illicit affair is exciting. Meeting in dark lounges for hurried drinks, holding hands in parking lots, brief encounters in small hotels—all the sneaky thrills of stolen love. And all the benefits of a backstreet wife.

After the courtship and consummation, the affair gravitates to your apartment. At first the candlelight dinners you cook have the aura of a honeymoon; dirty dishes at midnight give you time to recap thrilling moments of the evening. But then as dedication wanes, cooking becomes a chore, and sentiment vanishes. He can't marry you. The children, his financial involvement, her health, his health. He loves you but . . . You argue.

Trouble is, the more he demurs, the more you want him. What started with wine and roses grows ugly and banal.

Maybe you'll get an ulcer, but he won't.

It isn't worth it.

Oh, sometimes, if you are standing under a plum tree, a ripe plum may fall. But most of the time you get plummed in the eye. Even if he does decide he can't live without you, and he does leave his wife and family, friends, and long-standing ties, the wounds you cut along the way heal slowly.

The hurt begins when you put your hand in his. I don't think it ever ends.

Marjorie has a married lover. She's been sloshing around in surreptitious love for five years. He's been promising to leave his wife for three. He buys Marge little gifts, takes her children riding, showers her flowered sheets with vasectomized semen and goes home to Mama. Frustrated Marjorie cries, holds her aching stomach, beats her little hands against the wall, swears she'll never see him again —and then waits beside the telephone that same night for his call.

A very bad scene.

Judith's lover is older than she. Right after he promised to love her forever, he took a beating in Wall Street. Naturally, his losses held up the divorce proceedings. Then he had a heart attack;

but he lived, and she loved him even more. Naturally, a fellow confronted with possible heart failure can't fight about property settlements, alimony, etc. So, lover faded into his posh mansion.

There, with his rich and wigged wife, he lives out his days in dispassionate luxury. Sure, Judith forgot about him. With Miltowns, Valium, Doridan, and Seconal, there was almost no pain. In fact there was no feeling at all for a very long time.

You don't need it.

Though it's true that there aren't enough available men to meet current demand, still you've really got a better fighting chance in fair combat than undercover warfare. Hang in there. Stick to the probables and eventually the right man will walk out of the wings.

Lecherous and Loony

Before the ink is dry on the final papers you'll feel
a pat on the rear. Behind you, white hair gleaming in the sun, mouth agape with sensuous delight, will be Daddy Wishacould. He'll come to
call on Saturday afternoon with a quart of vodka
and orange juice and tales of financial wizardry.
Sooner or later he'll make his pitch; that is, to have
you render first aid to his prostrate prostate.

Don't laugh. It can happen. And more than
once.

The older the man, the more arduously he
seeks sexual rejuvenation. Ancient Greeks of vintage and esteem gathered young maidens into their
beds, believing that their youth and vigor would
be transferred by osmosis. Of course it didn't work,
but trying must have been fun.

Be flattered that the flutter of your lashes gives

the old fellows a boost. They understand when you refuse to invest in a bankrupt stock; even so, they keep on trying.

Once in a while a rich old Daddy ThinkIcan hobbles over to a practical Miss WhileIcan who waltzes him off to the preacher. Maybe it's not so bad. While he whispers "Sweet nothing" she scratches herself with that ten-carat stone. Some gals prefer limpo to hamburger haven.

It takes all kinds.

All That Glitters Isn't Class

If your natural habitat is the country club, don't look for a new Daddy at a truck stop. You're liable to find a brand that tastes good in the bedroom but chokes you in the parlor.

The old admonishment about similar backgrounds holds even more value in middle life. Moving up puts pearls on your neck but dropping down puts pebbles in your shoes.

Just admire those muscles when the garage mechanic changes your tire. When he asks you if you're married, say yes. Then pay your bill and leave.

A passionate love affair with a social or educational inferior can only bring pain and embarrassment to both of you.

Like we've said before, you don't need it.

And neither does he.

Go Alone

That old turkey, "Two's company, but three's a crowd" means boys and girls. Two girls are a crowd when one guy comes down the trolling track.

Even true on the golf course where courtship isn't always stifled by a foursome. If you are lucky enough to pick up a game with three men, jump for jolly pickings; the trio will forgive your fifty-two for nine and help you find lost balls like zealous beagles. If you're real lucky, one of them will be unattached (one out of three, never more).

Take the bus alone; walk alone; go to museums alone; browse in old Italian markets alone (bookstores, too); fish alone; skate at Rockefeller Plaza alone; ride trains alone (airplanes, too); yes, for Pete's (?) sake, travel alone. Shop alone, especially in men's stores, especially *haute monde* shops like Brooks, Saks, Neiman Marcus.

Get to know *you*—and maybe a few others along the way. Art galleries may appreciate your taste and your list of friends—if you go alone. The Metropolitan, on a springtime Sunday in New York, is a magnet for lonesome and cultured men. If he isn't there, so what! Renoir and Titian are!

The female twosome is out of date. Only one occupation to avoid—solitary drinking. It looks bad (except on trains, boats, and planes), and it can add up to trouble over the long haul. Some bars have that cozy back door that allows a lady's entrance without embarrassment, but to repeat, if you're over thirty, be prepared to cringe. At least at first.

If you go alone, you can leave alone, or with someone else, without responsibility for another.

If you have an invitation to a cocktail party, don't bug the hostess to let you bring a friend. A male friend, yes, but leave the girls to their own cocktail parties. Be generous, be helpful, but don't be crazy.

Never share invitations to parties or men with your female acquaintances. Even if they hem your skirts. You can make jelly for them or teach them how to tat. But don't introduce them to your men friends.

One man leads to another. It's the old chain game, and giving one away just breaks the chain.

Oh, you might give up old Derrick, after three months of Dullsville and no parties or exciting nightspots. But chances are if you don't dig him neither will your sidekick, and so you don't turn out to be a heroine after all.

If they do get chummy, he or she will eventually break it off; either way you come up the culprit.

Go alone to:

art galleries	nut shops
bakeries	orange picking
concerts	pet shops
department stores	Quebec
employment agencies	riding
fish markets	skiing
gas stations	traveling
hotels	Uruguay
ice-cream parlors	Venezuela
Jerusalem	walking
Kankakee	X-raying
Louisiana	Yellowstone Park
mushrooming	Zanzibar

If you go alone, you look like you need company. You really do arouse that old male protective instinct. Though it lies trembling under the attack of Women's Lib, it still manages an occasional foray to the defense of the feminine female.

Maybe you look hungry. One lovely *femme fatale* found a squire in the vegetables at the corner market. He asked if she would join him for dinner at the best Italian restaurant in New York. He thought she looked sad and hungry. And though he's been feeding her for two years now, she still looks hungry, but not sad.

If you go alone and there's a surplus (two) you get your choice. Too bad when you have a buddy and meet two buddies, and your buddy gets the buddy you preferred!

Of course, there are times it has to be Tweedle Dum and Tweedle Dee. A working girl's wages just won't cover single rates at a resort hotel. Same for shipboard. But if you do double up for economy's sake, split, for the sake of love, after you brush your teeth.

If you and roommate are on the American plan, sign up for separate tables; if she plays shuffleboard in the morning, you play tennis.

If you have a date for dinner and she doesn't, don't sweat it. She wouldn't for you. Tomorrow the sweat-er may switch. Being your brother's keeper doesn't mean to tag along with your sister and ruin everybody's evening.

It takes more than guts to strike out on your own. Without motivation, drive, and stamina, nobody does nuthin'. If you really plan to manhunt, be in top shape. (More about that later.) Come home, eat your dinner, rest for ten minutes, shower, dress, and jog off to that Spanish class or bridge tournament or gallery opening.

A girl friend would help to get you on your horse, but after that she would hold the reins.

Be inspired, crafty, creative—and selfish.

You can.

All the famous women in history were loners. Their salons were filled with men, but the competition got short shrift. Madame de Pompadour,

Germaine de Staël, Marie Antoinette, Queen Elizabeth I—all feted women in a world of men.

Today, making history, Jackie and Zsa Zsa follow this time-tested format.

So, go, girl, go—alone—and gather ye dingbats while ye may.

Sex and the Single (Again) Girl

On the Mound

It's a whole different ball game in a brand new ball park. And when you come up to bat you ought to know the signals.

Sooner or later, probably sooner, you'll find yourself half undressed, one leg in panty hose, the other out. Even if you haven't made up your mind, that heavy breathing in your ear means he has. If you fling yourself off the sofa and flounce away indignant, to the powder room, chances are he'll pull up his zipper and storm out of your life—forever.

There is nothing worse than two lipsticked, rumpled, rattled, unfulfilled subjects clutching wrinkled clothes at four in the morning. Only a foolish woman leads a man to madness and then shuts the closet.

You just don't do that anymore.

The rules are different.

However, the very first time you climb into bed with a man after your divorce, you will feel unfaithful.

To whom?

Ah, that is the question.

To no one of course. Except yourself.

But it happens. There is that unfamiliar naked body next to you. His hands have strong fingers wicked on your thigh. His mouth seems strange, kissing your sheltered skin. But then, suddenly, you forget to remember.

Sex has to have a place in your life. Women reach the peak of sexual prowess sometime around thirty, and they maintain this plateau of interest and ability to be aroused.

Women are better lovers than girls. They know men better, and they know themselves. They respond to a persuasive male time and time again. They learn how to play a particular violin, and how to prolong passion beyond infatuation.

More important to you, sex is pleasurable, exciting, and provides the most satisfactory psychic energizer yet devised.

Learn how to live your new role as a single (again) girl.

Appreciate the increment in your sexual abilities and enjoy. After you get over feeling unfaithful, and after the flood-like rush of guilt, you have some decisions to make. Immediately admit that though your new horizons hopefully include a marriage type mate, your present everchanging situation is what you have to work with. You, like 99.4 percent of your fellow humanoids, will have the urge to merge now and then.

He takes you out for dinner. He isn't bad, except for that capricious wink. He orders wine. The restaurant is candle-lit. His knee presses against yours, and he gives you the old intimate gaze. You know then, tonight is the night.

You've been out with him before—sailing one afternoon, lunch on a Wednesday at the Country Store, another dinner (good food, less romance). He likes you. His leg presses closer, and then his hand closes over yours.

You weren't born yesterday, but the operation's *avant-garde* as far as you're concerned! Well, don't hit the panic button. Just settle down, relax, let the wine warm your racing blood. Fight back your conscience and face the moment head high.

It might be fun. It might not.

But after three dates you ought to know whether he appeals to you *that* way. No doubt you've kissed him once or thrice, and he's probably put out a feeler or two himself. So you aren't really surprised. Though aroused, you hesitate. There are still the "What if's" inhibiting your sexual wishes:

1. "What if he doesn't like me?" Nonsense. He likes you already. You can feel the juices flowing in his probing knee.

2. "What if I don't like him?" So what? It's just a one-time mistake, and you'll forget. Just dance

him out, douche, and go to sleep.

3. "What if he won't go home?" He will. Remember? Men are just as sensitive about being rejected. They know when to leave—or stay. And if he won't exit, next time go to his house; then *you* can go home!

4. "What if he won't stay?" Unless he's married, he will. Even the most confirmed bachelor enjoys an occasional night of love, all night.

Whether or not the lady gets hot still depends mostly on the lady. That's nature, and nobody can change her rules. Jumping in the sack is a matter of your volition. You may be seduced (fun, fun), but you won't be raped.

If you like the way his fingers graze your inner arm (or thigh); if his tongue in your ear makes pimples goose from neck to toe; if he makes you breathless with a goodnight kiss, chances are— your chances are really good.

Reorientation — Right — Wrong — Rightwrong

There's always a "but," "however," or "unless" in the woodpile, isn't there? Of course, there's one here too. Once you get your sexual thinking reoriented and plunge headlong into ecstasy, you just might take your enjoyment too seriously.

It could *so* happen to you.

And as long as you had the right attitude (lighthearted) and cared for the equipment, it really wouldn't matter.

They could come and go and come and go.

But unless you fall victim to nymphomania, you will probably get the "come and go" blues. Which are:

"Why do so many of them come and go?" and then, "What's the matter with me? What do I do wrong?"

Nothing. Well, almost nothing. Maybe you're

too easy. And after your quaking conscience relents, you just might be. Pull in the reins. Slow down. Reach some kind of happy medium. You can't screw the world, and you certainly can't unscrew it either.

The "come and go" blues will go when *one* comes to stay. Until then, turn to cultural accomplishments one or two nights a week.

Boredom will slow you down soon anyway. Though the fine points of sex invoke more creativity than stitchery or cookery, there are other forms of stimulation. Orgasmic confrontation still sells better than the Beatles or Bach, but there's a lot to be said for holding hands in a good movie.

Everyone Should Take Driver Training

Love may be just around the corner, but then again, one detour, or six, or thirteen may be in order. It's best not to allow the machinery to rust or fall into disrepair.

Keep it oiled with the proper lubricants, and be sure to have a regular inspection. This means using a contraceptive, and having medical checkups every six months.

Your doctor may recommend The Pill, or maybe he's sold on the coil. There are still some gynecologists who opt for the diaphragm, but not many women. And there are no men, but none, who espouse the condom. They hate the things, and no wonder. They say the sensation is unbelievably frustrating, because there isn't any. It's like washing dishes with rubber gloves; you don't get your hands wet!

If a man uses a rubber, he's suspicious. It means either that he has a problem, or he thinks you have. And you know you haven't. However discriminating, clean, and experienced a man may be, he can still get caught some wild night. If you ever suspect that you may have run into a right guy who ran into a wrong gal, see your doctor. VD is very curable in early stages, and there is nothing to be embarrassed about. As your doctor will tell you, if he is honest, some of his best friends . . .

Again, don't count on a man for contraception. Oh sure, after you're his girl, if either of you have an occasional problem he'll fill in, but for openers, you're the (screw) driver.

Later on, when he's fast in love, you may be able to sell him a vasectomy. Painless, they are escalating in popularity and just may save the world. The operation, which seals off the small sperm-carrying tube from the testicle to the penis, is simple and brief. The results are ninety-nine percent dependable. But, until you are sure of your avowed vasectomized friend, use the coil or depend on the pill.

Now you've accelerated and slowed down, checked your chassis and added seat belts. But all new toys lose some of their luster after Christmas, and soon you'll find your zest for sex winding down.

You will become a gourmet. Quantity will cease to be your goal. Quality will determine your choices when fear and insecurity go away.

The Numbers Game

One problem. How many swallows do a summer make? How many affairs can you tackle at a time?

Two lovers might pass on a staircase, or meet in the elevator once too often. Keeping track of three could really be sticky!

Lots of veterans do have double-decked lovers. They establish rules for both one-and-only's, like MWF for Stan because of classes TTH; TTH for Bob because of classes MWF. Saturdays with Bill is wash day for Ron. Sundays with George is rest day for Tom.

In this tangled web, truth is stripped to the bone, and little lies blow up like fat balloons.

However, if you can handle such intricate dupery, and you like it as well, don't be put off by the less talented. They are, probably, simply jealous.

If your lovers bring presents (different nights, of course) be grateful. If they don't, get rid of them. There are no restrictive areas anymore. A red Camaro makes a nice middle-of-the-week offering; so does a king-sized opal.

But the ultimate bestowal in the courting game is that ten-carat diamond. And I don't know what the answer is if you get two of those on the same day!

Props for Preppies

If you plan to have even a moderately active sex life, don't invest in twin beds. Get a roll-away for family company, but commit your bedroom fortunes to a king- or queen-sized mattress. Doubles used to do the trick, but no more. Vitamins have made us all too big for singles, and our sex-vexed advertising has established the mattress as the playground of the world. Whether your playground is water, foam, box, or slab, make sure it's big enough—for two.

Use percale sheets. The difference in price is worth the smooth treatment your elbows and knees get. His too. Buy only wash and wear and change bed linens often. Unless you really do have a sex schedule, you never know when passion will appear.

Keep a supply of hand towels close by. Along

with Kleenex they're good for emergencies, planned or otherwise.

If you've been thinking about a man, and he breaks your reverie with a call, set the scene. Place decorative candles on the coffee table, desk, etc. Have the stereo at an all-night (romantic) station. Burn a little incense, even. And be sure you wear perfume. If you've splurged on pink (very feminine) satin sheets, take a minute to dress the bed before you dress yourself.

All set . . . just in case.

Have a good time at dinner; enjoy the show, and then invite him home for a night cap.

Light the candles and incense while he uses the john.

Turn on the music. Keep it low. Mix him a drink without asking. You know what he likes.

He'll recognize the props of course and love every seductive ploy.

He may think *he's* caught the lady moth, flickering in the candlelight. But you know who's caught whom!

Anyone for Scotch

A hint for the tipplers—and the non. Always keep spirits around. A little libation warms any gathering. When your steady feels steady enough he will assume the task of keeping the cabinet full. Till then, be sure to maintain a varied supply, and while you don't need the finest, don't buy cheap whiskey. Many men are connoisseurs and equate the whiskey with the woman.

Should you cook dinner for him? Well-l-l, it depends—on whether you can cook.

Helen invited Jack for dinner. As a wealthy married woman, she rarely visited the kitchen, and she never lit the stove.

But she wanted to have Jack to dine.

The table was perfect, gleaming with polished crystal, china, and silver (salvaged from her former marriage). And Helen looked splendid in a Dior hostess gown. The menu was okay too. Shrimp cocktail, salad, green beans, baked potato, and roast chicken. The shrimp was precooked, salad precut, green beans canned. The potato was slightly underdone, but passable.

The chicken, alas, was rare.

Rare chicken is bloody and hard to chew. Old Jack was tuned out, turned off, and nauseated. He went home early—and hungry.

But most divorcées have had experience in the galley and should be able to whomp up a simple dinner with confidence. Unwed males love to eat and relish a homecooked meal. Be sure, however, that he has taken you to dinner once or twice before you invoke DD (Domestic Duplicity). And be sure to ask him his favorite dish, so he won't think he's getting your ex's. (As Jack was taking his leave, he leveled his gaze to Helen and asked, "Did your husband really like rare chicken?")

Bed and Board

EF or FF? (In case you're too young, EF means
"eat first.") That depends too—on how hungry
you are and for what. In other words, don't always
plot your moves. Leave a little room for miscalcu-
lation and happy accidents. (If his digestion is
bad, you'd better eat later.)

Turning Him On

Even if you settle for one lover at a time, or when you get them down to the one you want to keep, hang on to some of the discretion you have learned.

Don't tell your March date what you did or where you went with December's man. Thursday's child doesn't really give a damn about the logistics of his Friday competition. It helps *you* for him to know that there were and are others, but keep identities your secret.

Arouse a little jealousy now and then. But, like perfume, a little goes a long way. If you're really throwing out the net, arrange for him to see you in some posh place with two smashing escorts. Two, because it indicates interest but not commitment on your part; one might knock your vacillating suitor out of the ball game.

Another ear raiser is the mysterious phone call. It could be your maid checking next week's assignment, but all you have to say (in a husky, intimate voice) is, "Call me later, can you dear. I've got company."

Same line will do for your almost-serious suitor when he calls. Even if no one is really sitting on the sofa with you, those words whispered to him, *sotto-voce*, will suggest another visitor. Jealousy is a strange affliction. Too much can derail romance and none scratch initial success. Apply with restraint.

Most men disclaim interest in your former lovers, and then casually try to extract carnal confessions. They say that what happened in your past is of no import, and certainly *their* conquests can never be revealed. But who were you dating when . . . ?

Don't fall into their trap.

In spite of his protestations to the contrary, in spite of your divorced standing, he envisions you as almost virgin. So leave confession to the church, and keep quiet about previous affairs.

Tell him what he wants to know. That you have, naturally, had other men, and possibly they could be called lovers. But he, your hero, is so superior in tongue and touch and tactile skills that they are not to be remembered.

He'll believe you and be grateful. And his amorous prowess will prolificate. Which is what you both want anyway.

If, however, he asks you detailed questions

about your former sex life while you're in the sack, spin a sexy yarn. He may be looking for an aphrodisiac for the moment. After your whispered tales of sensual experience redouble his efforts, you can deny the whole thing. And ask for an affidavit to credit your vivid imagination.

Donna didn't know much about the erogenous areas of Emile's body, but she *had* read *The Arabian Nights*. Her talent for storytelling fascinated him as she recounted fantastic sexual exploits. He kept coming back for more. Through a thousand and one nights she intrigued and bewitched him with her voice, until, like the fabled king, he could not live without her.

If you are sidetracked into an odd discussion of previous experiences (in some half-smashed situation) there is one forbidden activity that you must never mention . . . the one-nighters, those brief encounters that left you feeling blue, used, and sinned against.

One, or a couple, or maybe three or four happen to all divorcées.

Shame and guilt gradually fade into passing time, but every once in a while, a rush of memory rekindles embarrassment.

Forget. For good.

They happen in the first flush of freedom, only because of confusion, insecurity, and fear. And the "right now" need to have someone's hand in yours. At the time and in the moment those reckless flings served their purpose.

But in the retelling they sound unwholesome.

Memories of former loves are often sad, a part of life's price for pleasure. Okay, if you must, divulge. But endure the one-nighter pain in silence. And in suffering, fight off recrimination. It's an old saw, but we all make mistakes. Count your blessings if you survive a drunken confrontation with no more than bad dreams or memories.

Forgive yourself for your mistakes, as you would forgive others for theirs.

When your lover swings off the bed and pulls on his trousers, hold up on the waterworks. Men really hate to see women cry. It makes them feel powerless and incompetent. They don't know what to do. So they do nothing, and fear being exposed to that helpless feeling again.

So no tearful goodbyes.

Smile when he departs, as well as when he arrives.

Though your hands tremble as he knots his tie, it's best to looked pleased and unperturbed. He leaves a sanctuary of peace and passion, and by the time the elevator reaches the lobby he'll wish he were back. Cry after he leaves. Or better, not at all.

If you are one of the pessimists who just knows he'll never be back, keep that premonition to yourself. He doesn't know, and it's best not to give him the idea. Any indication of weakness on your part gives him the upper hand. If he thinks you worry about the frequency of his calls, or dwell on him three-quarters of the day, his pursuit of the quarry (you) will lose excitement.

It's always better to let *him* worry. Good advice but difficult if not impossible to follow. Strangely enough, suffering is half the fun of an affair. (The one who suffers the least loves the least.)

If he doesn't call the minute he said he would, wait a little while. Actually, men like to get phone calls from girls, but a too-anxious *inamorata* may turn him off.

Struggling through a couple of lost calls beats losing the caller.

Read a book. Write a book. Wash your hose. Go to sleep.

But don't call him too often. If his passion dwindles to a polite farewell, don't call at all. Your love might be refired by a ruse or two, but never by telephone histrionics.

If he doesn't call ever, go back to your little black book.

Women ought to keep a list of prospects just like their male counterparts. A man who plys you with drinks and compliments at a party when you're with another is always worth remembering.

He'll get a kick out of your first call. If you're lucky and he's on the loose too, he'll take the ball from there.

One last rule about phone calls. Don't blame a businessman for those he cannot make. If you work you will appreciate emergency situations that preclude fulfilling personal obligations. While you're waiting for that important jingle, he may be struggling with genuine problems.

Don't anticipate the termination of love by the

silence of a telephone. If he's any kind of a man, and he wants to say goodbye, he'll do it standing up, in person.

If not, talking to him is a waste of time anyway.

If your ego is trampled by a disappearing lover, you will simply have to wait out withdrawal. Symptoms are the same in every heartbreak. You cry and swear (at him), sit around in ashes and sack-cloth, gaze into space, and wish to see no one.

This, too, will pass.

If he turns out to be a disappointment after two months, just think how monumental your let-down would have been if you'd married him. Just a mistake, baby, and again the opportunity for new glamour and thrills to come.

Whether it takes two days or two weeks, your interest in the male half of the human race will be completely revived. Camille doesn't quite fit the pace of the times.

A broken heart might be a shade more tragic than a deflated ego, but essentially they belong to the same family. Foolish girls are not usually able to tell the difference; neither can their male counterparts. And after the affliction passes, whichever it was becomes even less apparent.

So open your little black book and try again. Better men are on the way if you can only wait.

Faithful or Never

When you are seeing a man in a sort of steady pattern, but with no spelled-out commitment, what kind of faithfulness is indicated?

Let your intuition be your guide, not your conscience.

Your conscience belongs to the old days. Today's barometer of ambivalence would never fit a Gallup poll. From not even looking into your doctor's eyes to switching dates at dawn . . . the gamut is ungaugeable. If you want to marry him and he measures love by loyalty, stay at home when his schedule is too full for you.

If he doesn't care, make your own guidelines. If you yearn for occasional honey from a different hive, spread out on nights when he's busy too.

Without a ring or concrete request, you're still your own woman. And he his own man.

And when one wonderful day he asks you the fateful question, you'd better be ready with an answer. If you hesitate, you hang his cool, and he'll remember two other girls he wanted to date. You see, men don't really like being kept in a stable any more than you like being one of a group. Even less. Their ego is more fragile. For the male bravado, that fake façade of impregnable masculinity disappears with feminine disparagement. He has a rough time getting back his self-respect. And once he's down, you're out.

By the way, most men *can* be categorized. Women, too, of course. But each romance makes its own rules. You write the rules. Just follow the norm and deviate according to attitude and altitude. If you know he loves you and you're flying high, feel free. You can (almost) do no wrong.

If you aren't sure and the buckboard stalls, try a different approach.

If you fail, forget it.

Disappointments bedevil even queens, movie actresses, and high-fashion models. At least your mistakes can be privately endured.

With or without a ring, once you have verbally accepted one man as the man, keep your word. His pledge is a promise, too, and you have a right to depend on that. No man owes you ice in August for the free gift of your body, but lovers who spell out their intent give up freedom for faith.

If either finks, honor goes out the window.

The End of An Affair — Their Way

What about the end of an affair?

Some have no real ending. Hands forget to hold, and nightly dates lose their thrill. The protagonists post notice that the affair is over. Usually mutual terminations of this type leave little bitterness. Relief is a common emotion, generally accompanied by respect.

Sometimes the parted lovers become friends; often one directs likely prospects to the other.

This is the best way to break off. There isn't much fire from dying embers; nobody gets their mainsail singed; nobody looks for solace. It's just over.

You don't get angry, because injustice doesn't enter into the picture. You can't really say goodbye, because the cutoff isn't definite. Two people simply disengage and go their separate ways.

Once in a while an undesolated duo use each other to fill in for dinners or coupled cocktail parties.

Sometimes ex-beaux go into the black book, too. In the "handy for emergency" division.

His Way

But then, there are the horrible upheavals. The ones that leave suicidal lovers in their wake.

The difficult withdrawal. Your resignation is signed per request, but indelible on the dotted line, the print of your heart remains.

The end of a love affair is terrible. Like the pledge to quit smoking, giving up a sweetheart requires support from friends and daily rededication.

You promise yourself not to call, and for a few days your resolve is Olympian. Then a finger stretches to his number, and the old magic wipes out the new will. His voice evokes happy memories and then more tears.

If he rejects you once more, for whatever reason, the call precipitates fresh agitation. You revert to those first days of panic.

No more appropriate postscript can be written

than "Goodbye. I love you, but goodbye."

Not knowing why he has left is hurt nonpareil. Summer fades away rightfully because change is nature's pattern, but accepting a lover's unexplained silence drains your strength more than physiological distress.

There is no immediate cure, no pill, no potion.

Death is less painful in its finality than heartbreak. Knowing that he sleeps two blocks away and buys groceries where you do is a terrible reminder that gnaws and doesn't go away.

Until a new man appears.

And you prepare yourself for another sweet surrender and perhaps another sad farewell.

But it's worse to lose out to the competition. Jealousy and remorse rage when you see Him with Her. It's then that your new escort never seems to measure up to the old, and you must inwardly bear the pain and anger.

And think he doesn't care.

Which he probably doesn't.

Your Way

Then we come to the farewells you inflict. When you empty the nets you've filled with one or more men you don't need.

Reasons for getting rid of a man for good:

1. The romance is over (for you, but he still hankers).
2. A richer suitor appears with Tiffany bait.
3. Revelations of his real self burn out passion.
4. He's married, and you see the light in his connubial window.
5. He loses his job and joins your check-of-the-week club.
6. He wears white socks.
7. He makes love with his socks on.

8. He divides his time between his mother, his Porsche, and you—in that order.
9. You find out the bracelet he gave you is fourteen-carat fake.
10. He chews with his mouth open.
11. He sleeps with his nose closed.

All very appropriate reasons for rejection. Any constant irritation rules out any possibility for continuing the romance.

You just don't want him anymore.

The first nasty word to learn is *NO*. Absolutely, positively, notwithstanding . . . NO.

No, you can't go to the movies, dinner, swimming . . . NO, no nuthin'.

Even if combat fatigue, boredom, and solitaire play havoc with your nerves—still the word is NO.

Once you've relegated a persistent suitor to the "forget it" file, forget it. Even if no other prospects are knocking at your door, say no.

Men are much better at the signoff job than women. They seem to have tune-out switches that allow no vacillation. Your tears turn their spigot to "off." Not all the time, but most of the time. So just say no if that's what you mean.

Tell him, like Caroline, that you just don't love him anymore. She returned his hammer, his tennis racket, and a pair of tickets for Radio City. Her suitor, in disbelief, appeared the following night for their usual date. His key still worked, but the night latch kept him out.

"Caroline," he yelled, "can't you open this door? I'm caught in your goddam crack!"

"No!" Nose to nose she glared through the separating links. "Turn in your key or I'll change the lock." He did, and she slammed the door, and the deed was done.

He knew she meant NO.

If he whines, smack him. He would you. Love doesn't have nine lives. Sometimes resuscitation works, but only leads to another noisier funeral dirge.

So a straight "NO" is the ticket. That way you control the rod, the line, *and* the hook.

Whether you are in the throes of seeking, enjoying, or curtailing romantic action, you are the boss. As a free woman you are (or ought to be) the mistress of your fate, within the limits of human control. Self-discipline is the single most important trait for you in the world of the new divorcée.

It's not a matter of what you're seeking, but the strength to withstand disappointment, the foresight to anticipate problems, and the intelligence to recognize success.

Trust your intuition. Have the courage to believe in your feelings and the guts to express them.

All you can be is wrong. Or maybe embarrassed.

Only giving women get. Put the real you on the line, and you'll double your pleasure. And if the flame glows only briefly, it still enhances your understanding and your warmth, the strongest assets of a woman.

Sometimes, when all seems lost, you can still get lucky.

Gloria tried and failed, and decided to forget Tony. After only two wonderful dates with her he found another girl. After three weeks Gloria sighed and crossed him off the list. Her interest turned to another.

Two months later Tony fished Gloria out of unfinished business and phoned. Available once more, he suddenly remembered their chemical affinity. She was delighted to renew the romance. And love was lovelier the second time around.

Sudden reversals are impossible to explain. When all is peaceful and serene, and the path of true love seems assured, a wordless and abrupt breakoff really hurts. But it happens.

Erica had a ring and thought she had Paul. Their relationship, begun in passion, progressed to a more relaxed stage. With or without her eyelashes, he loved her all the same. Their Sundays started with the morning paper and brunch in bed together, where they studied apartments for rent in the classifieds.

One weekend Paul didn't phone. He didn't drop in. He wasn't at home. He wasn't in the office on Monday, and they didn't know where he was or when he would return. Yes, the voices said, he would be back upon completion of a mysterious and lengthy assignment in parts unknown.

When no calls or letters came from distant cities Erica was devastated. She lost weight, and her face grew more drawn each day. No explanation eased her sorrow, as she mourned her missing fiancé.

Paul never reappeared. His image faded into a dreamlike memory for Erica as she rebuilt her life. She found a new love, and the roses came back into her cheeks. But even so, Erica still looks for Paul and wonders why he left and where he went.

Whatever the mind conceives can happen. Maybe Erica invented Paul, and maybe she made him disappear. Not likely, because Erica still had the ring.

But anyway, be prepared for shifting winds in matters of the heart. Don't be surprised to fall asleep one night loving Steve like mad and wake to wish him gone forever.

If you think it can be done, the power of your thought will work. Particularly for you. Weakness prevents accomplishment.

Be a winner within yourself.

And in the lulls between interludes, stock your larder with knowledge for new encounters. Read, rest, improve yourself.

Have confidence!

You can get rid of a kook or fashion a coup—*with confidence!*

All You Ever Wanted to Do About Sex But Were Afraid to Try

Reins for boy-girl activity were stringent when you were a girl. Freedom of behavior was limited and young callers carefully screened. Unchallenged in his role as protector, Papa upheld the ramparts of virginity.

You sat on a treasure that no dowry could equal. Each bouquet-bearing admirer knew who was available by the current tabulation. What you sat on was evident by where you went. Virgin or not counted a lot.

Not so today.

Some ministers espouse outside affairs in marriage. More condone premarital matriculation. Ladies' magazines that formerly rated imaginative cooking as their number one come-on, now sell meat loaf with sex. Plunging necklines have dropped to drapes around the waist, with talk about new bottoms imminent.

Morals depend upon the navigator, with mid-channel changes always likely.

Divorcées, once considered fair game by the waiting troops, have lost their unique standing. With the unmarried so eager to give away their wondrous charms, unleashed ladies become just part of the scene.

Much of the time between husbands is spent between sheets. You may fight for a while, but natural instincts are sure to supplant reticence.

Even in these permissive times, some meeting of the minds is necessary for the sensitive. Most women *cannot* climb into bed with a man until a mental rapport is established. Sexual intercourse is better after social intercourse.

Some men (and women) expect action on the first encounter. Most make no plans for such early activity, but look for ardor by the third date.

The best plan is to let the bells ring when they may. Let your goose bumps be your guide. And if you have a game plan that's undone with your bra, don't try to resnap the schedule. The sex syndrome and its consummation is almost old hat, but so far there is no replacement. Why not enjoy the best in this best of all possible worlds?

Maybe you need a drink to still your inhibitions or enhance your dramatic approach. Good enough, but gauge your tolerance with care. Though a slightly inebriated siren has appeal, a besotted sex scene is lead.

If he is a new lover, a drink or two might dissipate some of the strangeness. But water your whiskey and just have one. Better by far to pass up the booze.

What you wondered about so many years ago, you are free to check out today. The pockets of your mind are replete with forgotten sex questions from childhood. When you played doctor with all the cute little prekindergarten kids, some of your curiosity was satisfied. Everybody got to examine everybody, and the differences between boy and girl were duly noted and filed.

Further research for most female players was usually curtailed. As they matured, boys got to ferret out the "liberated" females. Most of them dallied with a few before matrimony got in their way. But our virgin-oriented society tried to de-sex the "nice girls" till they were safely tucked away on honeymoon lane.

The collision between knowing Tom and frightened Alice got the marriage off in a frenzied race—to failure. Alice, to her immeasurable loss, had been conditioned to keep her pants on, and she felt naked without them. What to do didn't come naturally, and naturally, Alice didn't come at all. Some of the more understanding spouses tried to re-lay the damaging groundwork before they planted the seed (mostly to no avail).

Twenty-one years of chastity had frozen the sexual urge. It took at least ten to effect a partial thaw. Sometimes the first eager penetration broke more than the bride's hymen. She learned to hate the act of love before she realized there could be love in the act.

One of these irate and unhappy victims was probably you.

You married as the iron curtain around sex was cracking. Kinsey's reports were our twentieth-century insurgence against suppression of natural desires. His scientific revelation of sexual statistics in the fifties relaxed barriers, swept away taboos.

Today Masters and Johnson have joined Freud and Kinsey as careful researchers opening the road to sexual understanding for the layman.

Sex is forever—because there is no substitute.

Sex provides the secret of renascence, of life.

Sex with love *is* life. And sex with love and shared ecstasy is more than life.

The key, for which we all search, is this combination of love and passion: intangible, undescribable, and not for sale.

The wondrous whole is rare, but bits and pieces mark our paths.

When some magic evening one eye catches another, a subtle hand glides down a silky leg, a bit of wonder awakens. You don't always know for sure, but your body gets the message. Western Union runs a sorry ninth compared to the rapid delivery of sexual stimulants to the brain.

When a playful hug soups up your motor, rejoice. Be glad that your nerves are alert and responses poised to react. If a tingle leads to a tangle you may get really turned on. And if the result doesn't equal the promise, at least you're making love—not war.

Getting into the sexual swing after years of conjugal restriction can be disastrous. Initial contact on the sofa may make you feel an overwhelming sense of guilt. Like gazing through a rainswept window, you get a distorted view of where you are going and why.

In trying to get a fix on your mounting frustrations and sense of physical failure, you may overload your circuits. And blow a fuse.

Promiscuity isn't the answer. Neither is celibacy.

The approach to sexual stability is rocky all right, cobbled with broken stones. But don't give up. You *will* get there. Drive "right on" through indiscretions, humiliating mistakes, and nice surprises. Maybe there isn't a pot of gold at the end of the rainbow, but hopefully, there will be a rainbow.

When controls have switched to "on" for both of you—it's time to enjoy. Let your hand linger in his on the way home (his or yours). Let adult gusto gather strength.

You know him at least a little. You like the way he smells (important) and the way black hairs cover his knuckles and the back of his hands. You like the way his eyes unbotton your blouse.

Relax. You've kissed him before, but only *his* tongue explored your mouth. Once you find what fun it can be, you too will be a spelunker. And when you taste and probe along with him his pleasure will be apparent.

Relax. When rippled nipples stiffen in his hand, hold your breath and enjoy your sexational response.

And if your fingers should just brush his rising

penis, pulse rate for both of you will intensify. A drink to precede seduction, perhaps, but long enough before the ultimate act so any alcoholic stupor will fade. And no further liquor to improve your bedside manner.

Love accelerates response. Even first loves bring nuggets of knowledge to the ignorant. But sex for fun (only) *is* fun, though it requires some sophistication. So you don't have to be in love to enjoy making love.

Before your sexual regeneration try to read Dr. Reuben, or the more formidable Masters and Johnson. Though yesterday's yearnings motivate your reintroduction to sex, today's knowledge will enhance your appreciation.

Most important to success in the sexual arena is to accept your right to be there.

Kissing is an art and your tongue a wild inflamer. What's more, all those quivery membranes in the perineum are meant to bring you pleasure.

New thinking diverts sexual gratification out of the sphere of wedded bliss into the common market. In any setting achievement of orgasm is truly the only physical ecstasy available to mankind.

Tennis just doesn't compare. (And isn't there always someone for tennis?)

Next to sex even dining rates a lesser role. And, of course, you dress for tennis, or dinner. There's also a pattern for office appearance. The outfit lends credence to the action, even unto bedroom sets.

So . . .

If you are planning midnight amour, why not appear in lace, preferably black. There are few men who won't respond to the lure of softly veiled curves, and his reaction will make you feel deliciously wicked. If black just isn't his bag, try periwinkle blue or innocent pink. At any rate, floating about in chiffon keeps your image sexy or sweet, or maybe both at the same time.

Whichever color casts the spell, buy the best. Though exquisite peignoirs cost like they're spun from dollar bills, they seem to last forever. Remember, they only appear in the first scene. After that, really, next to daring nighties, most men like skin.

Yours next to *theirs*.

Bodies should be satined with depilatories, kept smooth with sweet-smelling balms. Deodorants don't sound romantic, but they keep you that way. Use them to protect your Shalimar, here and there, and trust those TV experts.

Part of your survival kit is a good night cream. Use it freely on all alone nights but never when he's around. A too slippery track could derail the train! And most men really have an aversion to oily faces.

(Note here: Your cup runneth over with anointment for two. Scented baby oil provides a really fast freight; take care.)

Preparation for lovemaking includes pedicures and manicures, as well as expert handling of your hair. Only clothes look good half off—not nail polish. Beautiful fingers ought to flank a beautiful hand, and pretty feet need attention too. Devote a night a week to the care of your fingers and toes. By the way, fake nails look silly lying broken on the bed. Grow your own. No glue withstands love's wild abandon.

Hair can be a major problem. Only if it's long and straight or short and curly can you eliminate rollers. Usually not then. The rationale of good hair grooming is in the cut. A talented barber and regular shampoos assure rising from the pillow with heady confidence.

Keep trying for a great stylist. They're difficult to find, but once in your stable of services nonpareil, that's that. Don't change from hairdresser to hairdresser; you lose your place in line, and the line of your hair gets lost.

Men like lengthy tresses spread across a pillow (okay for under thirty) ; and for a nifty knot that, loosened, falls to your hips, an extra point or so. But hair is best bouffant and bouncy, soft for him to touch and stroke.

Teasing means to tantalize. Do it to your lover, not your hair. Back-combing after bed roaming looks like Halloween—so don't. And wigs! They can really scare off a likely male. Unless you look lovely beneath the wig, don't wear one. It just might come loose from its moorings in an unexpected encounter.

Now you're gowned and combed, lathered, perfumed and powdered, and ready for love. If he's aware of the preparations, by now he's bored, and the party's over. Pre-sack care is always preferred, but do the honors before he arrives. You can always touch up during intermissions.

Now enjoy! Don't sit there, hands folded in your lap; don't look little lost sheepy. *You can* enjoy making love. It's your right, privilege, and should be a pleasure.

Desire starts upstairs. A subtle touch on a distant toe sends messages to the brain for swift response. If your attitude is relaxed, you have an unending capacity for sexual fulfillment. The same potential exists within all of us.

Only the ability to realize that potential varies. Relax and you'll ring the bell.

Repeat again: if a drink dispels your hangups, have one with him—in your nightie. Suppose he does a little exploring while you sip; just close your eyes to savor every reaction. Won't hurt for you to get a hand in somewhere, too.

You don't have to be in love. For more than an evening.

He's alone and so are you, so why should you be celibate? Kiss him. Tip the back of his lips with your tongue. Draw his mouth to yours. Cool his ear with blowing whispers.

Undo a button in his shirt to slide your fingers through. Take your time. Remember the Chinese water torture. Prolong the prelude; let anticipation work for you.

He'll caress you, too, of course, and with narrowed eyes assess your escalating passion. Don't be shy; let him know what you like. Your reaction is his barometer; his excitement grows as you approach ecstasy, your pleasure a tribute to his masculinity.

Though he's caught up in his own passion, he'll remember next time what aroused you.

Pleasure begets pleasure. Yours, his; his, yours.

If the action begins in the parlor, it will soon progress to the bedroom. Let him be the initiator and drop your draperies on the way.

Atop the cool sheets let your senses pyramid to exhilaration. Listen: Hear his thundering heart and rapid breathing in your ear. Look at his body: strong, beautiful, and masculine.

Don't be afraid to *really* look. He is proud of his genital apparatus, his slender thighs and muscled arms. He wants you to say that you like the way he feels and looks.

His nakedness will add to your total sexual excitation, along with his particular smell and the taste of his skin.

He will touch you, and you must touch him. Your hand will act instinctively if you don't hold back natural inclinations.

In the beginning sex energy is diffused.

Erotic impulses emanate from all parts of your body. Each erogenous area telegraphs its delicious message to the brain. Each sensation stimulates mounting response, all building toward final ecstasy. If you lose yourself in what you are doing, culmination of your joint efforts will result in that fantastic neuro-vascular discharge known as orgasm. It may happen for both of you at the same time; it may be consecutive. The first time, for you, it may not happen at all.

Only because you didn't let it.

After a half hour passes or even before, he may want to try again.

This time your disposition will be less timid. You might even make a few suggestions to enhance your climax. When you become aware of your ability to reach the same plateau as any other woman, relaxation becomes easier.

Doctors maintain there are no frigid women, but that internal rebellion might interfere with orgasm. Anger against one or all men is sometimes expressed by consciously or unconsciously restrained emotions. Some Machiavellian wives withhold bedroom privileges to achieve their heart's desire; turning to the wall, their ardor waits till tolls are paid and banked. After the pay-off, orgasm for them is probably faked. As a matter of fact, a feigned climax with an old friend is okay now and then. If his ego depends on your accomplishment, you can bolster his confidence by pretending.

Don't feel discouraged by occasional failure. The female mind is easily derailed. Often she can't quite make it. Men are more direct in their advance, their mental gear less apt to wander from the scene. Some of them, the really caring, will know that you are not along; these unusually attuned men will persist until you, too, have reached the peak.

Don't envy nymphomaniacs. They can't always

make it either. In fact, their parade from body to body indicates a strange kind of failure in this department. As soon as any relationship with a man becomes more than casual they cannot achieve orgasm. For whatever reason, their brain refuses to cooperate, and they must move along. Though they search for the perfect lover in the sex game, their search, from the outset, is doomed. The perfection they desire locks their own mechanism. Usually, they cannot climax with the same man more than once. For you, a first-time fulfillment means more.

Expecting too much initially almost guarantees climactic failure for the gentle woman. Allow a couple of shots (blanks) to achieve a comfortable relationship. If he turns out to be a dud, lose him. Don't brood over disappointments.

Prepare yourself for sexual realization by becoming familiar with your equipment. This is no anatomic manual, but they *are* available in tiny capsulated versions or massive tomes. The more you know about your engine, the more satisfaction you will receive. Like using an electric blender, the mixture will be better if you know what knob to push.

If climax failure haunts your bedtime, get a vibrator. You've probably had one around for years to massage your tennis arm. Try it lower down. Electric stimulation of the clitoral area results in quick orgasm. Frequent use of this handy gadget should condition you, a la Pavlov, for the real thing. Motor reflexes are so speedy that you quickly learn to recognize the onset of total response. The vibrator has a salient effect on him also. If he's willing, experiment on him, too. He'll appreciate all your imaginative moves.

Don't be afraid to approach erogenous areas in new ways. Remember that making love affects your whole body and the uses of all its parts. Oral sex, if acceptable to both participants is perfectly okay, sometimes most desirable. For the so-called frigid woman it can help immensely in moving her along to almost immediate orgasm. If you like cunnilingus, don't feel sorry for your guy. Mouth genital stimulation excites him too. You do taste and smell different in that area, but the distinctive flavor is arousing to the male.

Try to erase your early (un) sex teaching that no sensual activity is acceptable except for procreation. You may also participate pleasurably in fellatio—lollypoperation for the fella. The salty, not unpleasant taste you experience is the same he gets from you. If he has trouble achieving a really firm erection, oral stimulation will almost always put him over the top.

It all depends on how you feel. About him, about sex, about you and your freedom to partake. Don't attempt to be what you are not, but do try to become what you would be.

Promiscuity is proof of nothing.

One man and one woman is all it takes to produce a sexual phenomenon, a lasting realization of sensual gratification that is right and good and fun. Fulfillment is . . . fantasia.

Any deep emotional disturbance will preclude a happy sex life. Recognize that frigidity is a sign of some malfunction and see a psychiatrist. Freedom of the sex ego is worth any amount of time spent on his couch.

The magic ingredient for successful lovemaking is in the atmosphere—before, during, and after.

When puddles of perspiration are all that's left of fevered ardor, don't run away. This is the moment for tenderness; the taming of a man is in the timing of a woman.

Whisper happy drowsy nothings; rub his back; kiss his hand and face. Cuddle. Coo. Mutual depressurization is wonderful on its own level.

If a nap escapes you, make him a drink or coffee, or even a bite to eat. It's the right time and a nice time to be hungry. After the first total exhaustion passes, watch television or talk. Then lead him out as you led him in. Be gay, pleasant, and poised.

Never register distress when he reaches for his trousers. Granted this is the worst part of the unwed act, but if he doesn't mind, why should you? The party is over for the time being, and he must go home. If the prelude, overture, and finale were a smash, he'll be back for an encore.

Remember to weep *after* he leaves. The script calls for a peaceful parting, even if you hate to see him go. And no lingering goodbyes; a brief farewell completes the plot.

Lean against the door and sigh; undo the rumpled nightie; wash the dirty glasses, take a bath, and go to sleep.

Wake up clean and glad. No regrets, guilt, or recriminations—you, too, are part of the "plumeless genus of bipeds" (Plato), and making love is temporal.

After a series of experiences in bed, your fears will vanish, your confidence increase.

But in the gaining you may lose.

Promiscuity is not the issue, but rather sophistication. You will cease to be wide-eyed and awestruck. Your acceptance of sex is sure to end your naïve charm.

After initiation you may become initiator. Some women, physically desperate, propose bedding down with men. Frustration releases all inhibitions for these unhappy scenes. The ladies name the plays in addition to the players. Seduction passes to the distaff side.

Men don't usually like these unfeminine forays.

They don't want their women to rule the roost or orchestrate the rooster.

Don't let this happen.

Ladies, let the gentlemen take the lead. You can stoke the furnace, but in the hay let him call the shots.

Women's Lib has its points, and women *should* get equal pay for equal work. But when man gets top billing in bed, woman collects the benefits.

A word to the wild is sufficient.

In your new and continuing venture into sex you can really try it all now. No one will know, and if they do they really won't care. Beware the perverts and the effete, the dumb and the contaminated, the indiscreet and the callous.

Everything you wanted to do about sex but were afraid to try is there within your reach.

Love can create its own lambent light.

Gone With the Winner

The Day He Got Away I Was Outside Hanging Up Clothes

Losing isn't much fun. After a valid investment of time, creativity, intuition, and persistence, it's sad to find the romance ended—by him.

Disappointments can overwhelm the divorcée.

Hard enough on the confident single, loss of a lover brings desperation to the suddenly abandoned lady. Added to the trauma of divorce, rejection by a man cuts deep. Even after common sense and a new alliance mend injured feelings, scars remain.

The immediate embarrassment is almost menopausal. Hot and cold flashes accompany memories of the flimflam.

Like a shark on a shoal you feel exposed.

But the world isn't watching really.

You're still just one of many.

Hot Treatment

Betty was an attractive brunette, age thirty. Divorced only a few months, she hated living alone. Although her calendar was studded with dates, her spirits tailspinned. She only wanted *the* man, and he was nowhere to be found.

One happy day a brilliant lawyer came into Betty's office. A mutual friend had described her in such glowing terms that he couldn't wait to see for himself. The outgoing attorney was reasonably tall, exceptionally handsome, and very rich. He played tennis, liked boating and bedding. So did Betty.

It was noon when he was announced, so they went to lunch. Laughing and flirting and holding hands, they appeared to fall in love.

That night they danced under make-believe stars and floated in that ethereal atmosphere where only lovers fly. Supercharged, their antennas vibrated wildly, and they just made it into bed. Even here their physical enjoyment matched. His farewell was tender, and both of them hated to say goodnight. It looked like a long happy summer ahead.

"Tomorrow noon," he whispered.

But the next day brought a distressing message. Betty's amorous solicitor called her office. He told her secretary that he couldn't keep their luncheon date.

"Tell Betty hi," he said casually, and hung up.

He never called again.

Betty was totally confused. And since the lawyer was part of the business scene, she had to face embarrassment each time they attended a meeting together.

To this day she wonders why. Set up or impromptu, his treatment left Betty distraught, her ego shattered for a long, long time.

Cool Treatment

Many a luckless gal is led astray by a sweet-talking man. Best advice is not to let a line become a lasso.

Ellen wanted very much to believe her brand new friend. Barry was a slicker, even in the city. The combo was perfect for him, poison for her.

He had a pattern, and she followed it.

On the first date he told her she was adorable. "You're adorable," he whispered as he toasted her with wine.

"You're adorable," he sighed as they bossa novaed.

"You're adorable," he said, mussing her hair and kissing her mouth.

Then the silent treatment for days.

Ellen succumbed. *She* called him.

He was waiting. "Let's have dinner . . . tonight."

Anxious Ellen took the bait. She had dinner with Barry and a night cap at a fancy saloon. Then he nibbled her ears and whispered "adorable" all the way to his pad. Conquest complete at 4:00 A.M., he managed a final "adorable," flipped cab fare onto the bed and fell asleep.

Angry and deeply hurt, Ellen ate crow for a month. Barry's still catching strays, but once-eager Ellen has learned to be cautious.

Disappointments are bad in another way. Aside from being embarrassed, your overall picture of men gets blurry. Cynicism settles in, and, like milk, cynics sour. Don't let one or two rotten deals spoil your taste for anything but rotten dealers.

Sometimes a schemer will fall into *your* web. Under your influence, he may mend his ways for a while, but if you hook a con man be wary. His tactics may be great as a temporary lift, but unless you dig the cheat scene, keep looking around. He'll still think you're adorable.

The Un-Caller

Why don't they call back? Who knows? Suffering flowers brood endlessly over this dilemma. At least the abused male has the chance to hear you say no. Of course you can call, but it's better for you to wonder, speculate, and forget—quietly. Why let the rotter put you down? Just rip up your tickets and step up again. Everybody has a winner once!

Sometimes they do say farewell. Evelyn was treated to a flattering good-bye. She was surprised but pleased when a special friend announced his exit. Aware that their future held little promise, she thought it was nice to know.

"Fred," she said, "I'll miss you. But I'm glad you've finally found *the* girl."

"If we'd met sooner," said Fred, "it would have been you."

Evelyn resented this parting dig from a square, but appreciated his farewell. As a matter of fact, Evelyn's loser turned up a winner—for Evelyn. Fred introduced her to Alex, a recently widowed, unhappy friend. In six happy months Ev married Alex, and *she* was saying adieus to former dates.

No one can say what whim knocks a prize over and out.

When the course of true love grows bumpy, then breaks off altogether, hearts mend slowly. But when an infatuation fails, recovery is quick.

Disappointment is very taxing but not lethal. What's more, you learn a lot from your mistakes. After a few false starts, the budget starts to balance. And so do you. One conquest will outweigh three flops.

A strayed boyfriend really isn't such a setback. And when contented husbands can be tempted, it's nothing for a new suitor to be lured away. Of course a novice is bound to be outflanked by more experienced players at first. But after a month or so in the field, you too will be stealing boyfriends and dumping stiffs. It's a serious game, and a gamble, like living.

For the divorcée, who's already wasted a lot of time in court, renewed courting is grim. At first the lonely lass feels an urgency. Hoping to find a safe haven she falls into any arms. But time tempers fear. She begins to recognize the specials, to distinguish real men from phonies, learns from each mistake and finally, how not to make them anymore.

Strength is made, not born. Every single (again) girl has got to earn her stripes. Disappointments fill the memories of heroines who find more than one lover gone with an unexpected winner.

Love

What is love? What is this most treasured emotion that bedecks the halls of history? Concocted by witches, embroidered with blood, strewn with wrecks, stained with tears, utterly confusing, love is being happily unhappy. You can't see it or smell it or taste it, hear it, feel it, or have it, except at the whim of fate.

Laugh and the world laughs with you; cry and you cry alone, but for love the number can only be two.

Though poets speak of love and its accompanying rapture, they also sigh and sing of pain.

Love is chained to hate. An irate lover is a volatile protagonist. Conversely, overwhelming compassion is love's twin emotion; what hurts one partner is painful to the other.

Certainty is not a facet of love. Until the lovers

are wedlocked, jealousy makes waves, and insecurity troubles both sides.

Love is war.

It's wanting what you can't have, winning or losing, then sometimes getting what you don't want.

Falling in love is fun. Excitement gives you goose bumps; anticipation rises with the sun. Little things suddenly mean a lot; picnics with ants, pebbles in your shoes, holding hands. The mundane becomes profound. Stars that never hung around before light up the heavens for lovers, only lovers.

Falling out can be terrible. Unrequited love sometimes wrenches the mind from its moorings; suicide and murder are not uncommon catastrophes when lovers part. Melancholy babies brood and mourn after the end of an affair.

But, most of the time, falling in and falling out is achieved with no more than temporary dismay.

Youngsters, in the wonderful stage of learning to live, move from crush to crush. Each flower is sweeter than the last. Old scars from scuttled loves build strength for later, more important bouts.

Adults survive on strength gained in these sophomoric rituals.

Real love, with no more identifying marks than first infatuation is difficult to recognize. It doesn't often happen in a day or a week. It doesn't come when you expect it, and yet, somehow, in spite of fights, misunderstandings, and setbacks, real love hangs on.

Love is more than "not having to say you're sorry." It's never having to be sorry. His love plus your love is ardent and equal and facile. Love plus love is love-love and wings away to the moon. The greatest treasure on this spinning globe is the least costly and the most rare—love-love—love-love—love-love.

If you think you've found it, trust your feelings. The most experienced sackmate cannot attain the reaches of love-love, while with the right partner (trained or not) you can conflagrate the couch.

There is no prescription, and reason is no guide. The barometer exists only within you. You can seek psychiatric help or cry on a friend's shoulder, but you have to recognize love-love on your own.

Falling in Love — Overage in Grade

After thirty, falling in love isn't easy. Faults appear as permanent traits in the opposite sex. A prospect in his best years (twenty-thirty) is usually flexible, but from there to sixty the dwindling supply of men become more difficult to handle.

Set in their ways, they resist change. A bomb might unsettle their entrenched routine, but a new love, or even a true love, would have to conform to their habits.

That's important data for divorcées. To change him is a challenge, all right, but one not worth the effort. You wouldn't want much modification yourself, even though you may vary your first efforts just to get into his groove.

So you have to work with what is there, not what might have been. If he's color blind, of course, he'll appreciate suggestions—before he's dressed and in the car.

That's the only revision a man will invite, and most men aren't color blind.

There's little hope that you can change his way of chewing, talking, dancing, drinking; or his choice of church, clothes, whiskey, movies, or politics. He may smoke your cigarettes when his are out, but on most matters his mind is made up.

If you have a set program planned, forget it; don't base the future on what seems to be perfection. You won't have to wait long for his reversion to old habits when you are won.

Watch the men over forty jiggle their jowls when they talk. Though the hair is just half, the sideburns are all gray, and sometimes the sideburns are all. Not quite decrepit or crippled or ill, each ails with minor maladies—here and there.

In that department you too show signs of maturation. You may be approaching thirty or forty or just around menopause (fifty), which causes you to be often irritable, cranky, or unreasonable. Your face may have sagged a little too, and don't those frown lines bother most women!

Looking older is the price to stay alive. The payment can't be postponed or charged to someone else. But, happily, the downward sag doesn't lessen passion. Man's physical deterioration moves slowly on the mind, emotions, and pleasure factors.

You are never too old to fall in love.

Whatever your physical expectations may be, however, remember that hopes for renovation are unreasonable. After thirty both men and women are wearier, less impulsive, and wiser. Learn to love him in spite of the signs of fading youth, and hope that he will do the same for you.

A little dyspepsia doesn't kill the appetite. So don't be alarmed at the run-down candidates who arrive in the rush. Most everyone over thirty has a curve in the belly. Skinnier legs and bigger chests add to slightly unbalanced dimensions. Except for ectomorphs (thin guys) and athletes, the middle-aged men you meet won't be shaped like leading men. But, to repeat, neither are you!

Give the man a chance. Even if he's bald or bent or a little too old. Remember:

> Although the hair on top looks like snow,
> A fabulous fire may burn below.

Sometimes it happens quickly. You meet, hit it off, and then sizzle. The declaration of dependence is inevitable and merger is immediate.

But love doesn't usually develop so fast or come to a head so readily.

Most shoppers are unsure. They shift position, hesitate, and stall through the various stages of emerging whatever.

The first date is the hardest. If it's a blind arrangement there is double reticence. The gentleman doesn't form an opinion right away, but the lady likes to think *she* knows from the moment he steps into her parlor.

The shape of his head or the angle of his pipe is enough to forecast the pattern. Unless you are a dingbat with a face like a bull, however, the man will give you a gallant look and withhold judgment till later. His expectations are less than yours. He feels lucky not to get a witch. You, on the other hand, know Paul Newman isn't ringing the bell, but until the first look, you hope.

You'll know if he likes *you*. After that initial tooth-gritting greeting his physical and spiritual totality will come through the door.

If you like *him*, show it. Smile and meet his eyes.

Although men register some anxiety towards blind dates, most are willing to gamble. Their anticipation isn't for love but a reasonable facsimile, and every lady looks hot till proven not.

A lasting alliance can come from a temporary liaison. Don't avoid sophisticates because you are shy. He may be tired of the faster types, and your moderate speed may be just the refresher he needs. Slower men could be winners for you too; so occasionally try the tortoise and pass the hare.

From that point let him be the leader. If you are reluctant he will be eager. But indicate your approval of his approach.

Be affectionate. Most men echo the warmth of a woman. They love sudden warmth—touching, kissing, holding hands. When you reach, they react, and their pleasure is apparent. Love comes from loving.

Believe in yourself and trust your feelings. If you find a common bond, prepare a feast.

Try to recognize the real, eliminate the fakes. At thirty no one is fearless. Only a youngster pulls the trigger without fear.

Payoff is the total package. It takes meeting, communicating, and that unpredictable affinity. Without the carton, the wrappings, and the ribbon, you don't get the beau.

TV for Two — When You Think
You've Got a Goodie

Problems really triple when you get to third base. Holding hands and almost home, you've got to make up your mind. So does he.

He might need help for the final hurdle. But then again *you* might reject the jump. Hot in the chase, the pursuer is certain he wants the pursued. But sometimes the pursued quits or is less alluring in the net.

Many marriages in the now generation happen after the lovers have lived together. With some, marriage is not mandatory. Maybe your misgivings preclude an official splicing. Maybe you want a promissory note and an extended affair.

After a year in the single state, you may covet your privacy and seek to preserve solitude. In spite of some apparent reluctance to live alone, you *have* been growing independent. You might just have *thought* you wanted to marry.

In any case, give old Gus another gander.

Is it easier the second time around? Some ways yes, some ways no. The new man's faults will differ from the old, and sometimes you may get the two mixed up. If misdeeds are the same, first hubby may get the blame, while the second resents the error in name.

Cuddling in the conjugal bed might lose appeal as soiled underwear and shirts fill your laundry bin. Only the youngest men on the market join the housekeeping jamboree.

Your old spouse left the chores to you and chance; the new one will probably be the same. This generation was phased in by unliberated Moms who believed in "men first."

So, don't expect second-time Jim to wash the dishes while you watch TV.

However, to give the darlings credit, some of them have learned to cook and love the culinary art. They will, at the slightest provocation, dirty every pot to come up with a dish you didn't want at all.

Most of them, weaned in a white-collar world, can't even hang a picture.

But don't get married to have a handyman. They're not that difficult to hire.

Marry for love, or marry for money, and do both or either slowly.

While you are deciding on marriage, don't mend his socks or iron his shirts. Even if he helps to keep the cupboards full, pretend you can't hear his

THE SENSUOUS DIVORCEE 129

household hinting. Oh, once in a while you can sew on a button, but don't be tricked into domesticity, especially before wedding bells, unless you want double duty later. All advice you won't heed, I'm sure. When a woman really falls for a man, she plys the needle and bakes fat pies—only to lose the bounder to a lounging shrew who doesn't know eggplant from peppers.

After you've fed him his favorite Irish stew and sewed the buttons on his coat, you'll probably have to listen to his problems. Danger here, too. You may become an ear for every little complaint (a bore). Discuss and analyze, okay, but don't be a butt for a bore.

If he starts to play the heavy, with secret overnight missions to Buenos Aires or Tel Aviv, knock off his bluffs. Remove his hat from your hook and show him the door.

Don't let the end of the chase mark the end of the charm—yours or his. Survival must follow success, and love needs constant attention. Connubial cohabitation is the toughest kind. Participants forget to keep the picture pretty; and familiarity brings on the blahs.

Whether you're official, semi-official, or common-lawed, don't let the courting die.

Dine out and dance once a week. Hold your body close to his. Touch him when his back is turned. Kiss whenever you can.

Get excited over presents. Show your appreciation with joyous hugs when he remembers a special day. Leave a love note now and then—tender and sweet. Scotch-tape a poem to the toilet top. Pin a sexy thought to his pillow. Silly? Sentimental? Maybe. But a real bell-ringer on a gray and rainy day.

The fragrance of roses means "I love you" forever. From woods or florist, posies show that someone cares. Wear them or bring them with a smile —for him.

Don't forget to remember to be all the things you were the week before. No rollers or scroungy robes, no dirty bras or sleazy slips. Keep your nighties fresh and your lingerie pristine clean. Hang on to some of the privacy and hope that he does the same.

Mystery spices monogamy. Keep him intrigued with new tricks. Try to fit in some travel. Making love in Peking, just for a change, could fire up your lover.

Penny Ways

The bomb that obliterates gourmet cooks and bedtime's sexiest babes is the dollar bill. When there aren't enough the whole team gets edgy.

Money matters create a bigger mess in second marriages, and it's best to avoid a financial fiasco, for sure. If you're both poor don't sweat. The penniless don't panic unless they get an unexpected slice of Gramma's pie. Still a system helps to prevent disaster.

If *you* have the money, don't part with a quarter till you're sure *he's* not queer or a quack—and that it's *you* he digs. A wealthier man, remembering a former settlement sum, will probably produce a contract. Thus, protected, another split will just separate him from you, not his cash. Most include terms for token alimony only, a fitting procedure for the formerly framed.

It's a puzzlement. Carefree and cautious is an impossible combination, but the only way to go. It's like riding a roller coaster while waiting at the gate, or racing through space on a pea-green spoon. Impossible. But at least you can try.

There isn't much chance that either of you will change, and lovers always scrap. The percentage is with the head of the house. Of those who marry for the second time, many are divorced again, with money the main culprit. Still, there will always be an urge for sex, and the paired-off population will continue.

Some make it the second time around, while others keep going around and around. Those who have a predilection for mistakes keep repeating them. Others learn their lesson, proceed with caution, and finally chalk up a winner.

Keywords:

No advice is valid unless you try it, and it's safer to sift for yourself.

Personals — Pie in the Sky?

Selling a business or buying a yacht is run-of-the-mill routine, but paying your way into the "Personals Column" is a ticklish job . . . especially when you hope to sell yourself.

At the classified counter, I filled in the standard form with what appeared to be cut-to-the-bone brevity:

> Woman-attractive—38 5'5" 125 lbs. to meet interesting man 35-55 for dining, dancing, sailing.

The clerk respaced my work, counted, and clipped, "Four and a half lines, which is really five, at $1.41 each. Okay?"

"$1.41 a line!" I was nonplused. "That comes to $7.05."

"Plus your box at $1.25. Total $8.30. Okay?"

"For a week?" I pursued.

"One day . . ." the girl paused, amused at my amazement, then volunteered, "It doesn't have to be so long, you know."

She capsulized my version to read:

> Woman-attractive-38 to meet man 35-55 dining dancing."

With the box, the two lines totaled $4.07. Grudgingly I agreed the content could not be further cut, and she wrote up the insertion order. "Many advertisers with this pitch?" I asked.

Laughing, she nodded. "Loads."

"What do they look like?"

"Mostly nuts in need of bolts."

"And the men. What are they like?"

She hesitated, cautious at my persistence.

"I'm writing a book," I urged.

"Oh, well . . ."—she shook her head—"not much to tell. No glamour boys of course; lots of fat guys and balding bachelors. Coupla winners with wigs, too. One fella asked me could I tell he was wearing one. I said, 'Nah . . . you look great!' But I could, because it was crooked."

The girl said that only a few use their own names. She guessed ninety percent were fakes. Most people ask to pick up their answers at the paper, even though mailing is mandatory. Smith and Jones are the favorite *nom de plumes*. Women are nervous and in a hurry. Unlike me, they rarely opt to change their ads, or voice resentment about rates.

Thursday afternoon is the big mate bait day, and rarely are the advertisements placed for less than three issues. Average length is three to five lines, though some run as high as ten, and cost is no consideration. My informant was not aware of any particular pattern of results. No one ever brought a wedding cake to the classified in celebration of a "media managed merger."

When I paid my bill the cashier agreed that most personals of this type did indeed cost more than mine, and wished me luck with my response. Then, handing me receipt and change, she smiled sympathetically. "I wouldn't think that *you* would have to advertise." I made a hasty, backward, embarrassed retreat, relieved to know the results would be sent to the privacy of my home address.

The ad ran on Sunday, July 4—maybe a bad day for roamers, but great for holiday pigeons at home. Two days later, seven answers arrived. The next morning eight more. Tabulation for the total was nineteen, plus a come-on from a computer guaranteeing perfect partners every time.

Most of the answers were handwritten. One included a brief note on scratch paper along with a formal résumé. Another attached a tiny photo. Handsome, he said he was a hairdresser and signed off "With love."

Jim dickered for dining, stressing his gourmet side.

Charles couldn't dance (on dime store stationery) but promised to learn, if I would teach him.

Sandy wrote a billet-doux, xeroxed the original, and mailed the copy. I guess he kept a file. One of two who included college in his background profile, Sandy's handwriting rated superior in the answer stack.

Bob said it like it was when he warned, "I've nothing to offer except myself."

Joe wished me the happiness I sought and signed, "Sincerely." I think he meant it!

There were no salacious notes and only one perverted letter. Will was no stereotype but a kind of offbeat Tarzan looking for his Jane. In pencil he wrote:

> Dear Attractive woman
> When I go with a woman I go with one I only do and care for her not two or three. When I go with a woman I go out of my way to please her only. If she is rude or naughty I will turn her over my knee and give her a saucy sound spanking. If you was my girl and you was naughty I would turn you over my knee and give you a saucy sound spanking. I would cover you with kisses from head to toe and tell you why I spanked you. The spanking would be for you being naughty. Then you would know you had a man that only cared for you. Don't you think a lady that is naughty deserves a good spanking I do. In closing it was a pleasure writing to you. . . .

Kelly used a two-inch cut of postcard with this enigmatic message:

> My dear Attractive woman:
> Your "ad" intrigued me—If you wish to find out about "us"—and learn more about "us" —call. . . . Perhaps we may have "charisma."

The least ordinary epistle was signed "Sarah."

> Madam:
> My husband and I would like to meet you or talk to you about going out to dinner and dancing. We are also attractive and 38 and we would like to meet you. You may call me at . . . at any hour. . . . Just ask for Sarah.
> Most Sincerely, . . .

Sarah is hardly a sinister name, but the meaning of her message was clear. A proposition from a pair was a surprise, and I couldn't help but wonder who would do what with whom!

I checked what addresses were available. For the most part they lived in shabby apartments with shaggy window shades on potholed streets. Clearly, these lonely hearts needed more than love.

Only two of the answers seemed worthy of pursuit. The script was sophisticated, the paper bonded, and content grammatically correct.

Addresses for these were also acceptable. "A" lived in a new high-rise—a chichi condominium. "B" docked his boat behind a small but trim little house in the suburbs.

The letter from Mr. Condominium was brief, informal, and to the point:

Dear Miss,
Your ad in today's paper interests me. Am unattached, in my late 40's and live alone at the address above.
You can reach me before noon, late afternoon, or after 11 P.M.
Will appreciate hearing from you in the near future.

Sincerely,
"A"

I called to see what appraisal I could make on the telephone. He came across gruff but literate, and with an ego that needed little inflation. My ad was just one of several he had solicited, but I could not induce him to divulge his other experiences.

I didn't like his voice, although I agreed to meet him for a drink sometime the next week. Later I changed my mind.

"B's" answer, however, was frank and homey. Couched in cautious terms he explored the possibilities of finding romance in the Sunday supplement.

Dear advertiser,
I have always been curious about personal ads but not enough to answer . . . at least until now.

Frankly I am just over 55, but feel the slight increase in age has not slowed me down as yet. I'm six feet tall, weigh 189#, own two homes, a candy business, and raise dogs . . . poodles. I am widowed, enjoy camping, sailing, and fishing, as well as dining, dancing, and pleasant conversation.

My telephone is unlisted. If you think I might be interesting to meet please drop a note to the above address. Either tell me where to meet you and when, or send along your phone number, and I will get in touch with you.

Sincerely,
"B"

I wrote a short letter enclosing my number, and when he called we arranged to have brunch at Howard Johnson's on Sunday morning. I took along a friend.

We both found him reserved, pleasant, and good company. After this initial meeting he phoned once or twice, but we never quite got together again.

"B" was simply a lonely man. He didn't fancy singles clubs or go to bars.

His response to me was less than lasting, though, and I doubt that he ever perused the classified columns again. But "B" *was* a plus for the Personal approach.

Most of the shadowy figures that lurked behind my nineteen letters seemed less than wholesome

—adventurous perhaps, but fraught with too many unknown quantities for me to worry about.

Pie in the sky? Mostly. Winners don't wait to be snagged by a one-inch newspaper snippet . . . However, like all other hazardous roads to love, who can tell? Maybe your next romance is in today's news, where the nameless drop anchor in a paper box. But really, the choices you get aren't worth the chances you take.

Then there's the other side of the search— the high-powered pitch of the advertising man. Even in the personals they preen their tails like peacocks:

> Unattached gentleman, 46, 6'2" good-looking desires dating attractive Capricorn, Scorpio gal over 5'3" between 28-40 dining, beach.

For serious cheating he spreads his feathers wider from behind the printed screen:

> Business executive youthful 40, 5'10", 170, wants fun-filled afternoon dates with personable girl 21-35 dining, fishing, etc. Discretion assured and expected.

To complete my research I answered one of the more extensive listings in a Sunday's paper:

> Recently retired Northern businessman, 46, 200 pounds, well read, well traveled, financially independent would like to meet very at-

tractive woman, 25-40 with fine figure, bright, witty, with sense of humor who enjoys dining out, theater, good music, stimulating conversation. Please reply in depth.

His advertisement was ten lines plus the box. I added up his tab, and it came to about sixteen bucks. This guy wanted a gal and could probably afford her. I wrote:

Dear Sir,

Your ad in Sunday's paper projected you to be intelligent and articulate. For this reason I have decided to answer briefly.

I am also well traveled, as well as knowledgeable in the arts. Most find me attractive and I have a sense of humor.

I have a dual purpose in answering your ad, which I shall explain should we have the opportunity to talk.

Realizing that there is an element of danger in a situation of this type I shall omit my full name and address. If you wish you may call at

In any case, good luck with your search.

I mailed my answer Friday morning. The phone rang early Saturday, "Hello there!" The voice was quick and bright. "I'm Frank Player. Thanks for your letter."

He was intrigued with my mention of double motivation and anxious to know what they were. I explained that I was researching for a book and would appreciate his reasons for using a classified ad to find feminine companionship. Frank was cooperative, though disappointed not to find me a candidate for his search. Though he claimed to live two hundred miles to the north, we talked for the better part of an hour. I never told him my name, and I am sure that his was an alias.

Once before he had advertised. On the first effort he was avalanched with fifty answers, contacted twelve and ended up with two super playmates for the winter. From this second "Personal" appeal he had counted eighty-seven seekers so far, among them four men who asserted that they could do *everything better than women!* Two prostitutes were tallied—prices listed and accomplishments logged. One practical lady (in a xeroxed letter) asked if he would keep her for a while so she could paint without financial problems. A p.s. to her proposition requested that he pass along her letter to another who might be interested if he was not.

Ages for the respondents ranged from late thirties to early forties. Few were literate, and not many filled the designated in-depth descriptions.

I asked why he chose this method to meet women. He replied that advertising avoided long and tedious searching for the perfect partner. An hour's reading eliminated the losers, the ambiguous and vacillating, the uneducated and stupid. Twenty percent was what he hoped to pursue on the telephone, where a further indication of intelligence would emerge. From ninety answers he might wind up with six or seven probables. Discreet rendezvous with this eight percent would probably net four or five "dining dancing" companions for a short term dalliance. Mr. Player was fun to talk to. He gave me a stock market tip and ended our conversation with a promise to call again, "just to chat."

Mr. Player was also married! Like all the knotted swingers, he claimed to be on the verge of divorce. To be fair he told each female on the phone that he was wed.

Mr. Player just wanted to play, and that is why his *nom de plume* was proper—and fitting.

Along with letters from people came a pitch from a computer. The envelope was self-contained with a foldout questionnaire. Applicant was to check multiple choice questions about personality and preference. Also requested was an appraisal and list of interests. For ten dollars an immediate and ideal match was guaranteed if you responded to all questions honestly and accurately.

The client need never appear at the agency to be serviced. All information was gathered and dispensed by exchange of eight-cent stamps.

Most former participants dislike the service. Results are rare. These assumed vendors of social contacts exploit the misery of lonely men and women. Computers offer promise but produce mostly disappointment.

Once in a while a match emerges, but the odds are with the house once more. Whether or not to try a computer plan is difficult to say, but in all likelihood your chances aren't very good.

Sally sent fifteen dollars in response to a classified ad. The company returned a form which she filled in and mailed back. Two days later she had her list of dates, and they supposedly had Sally. Her fifteen dollars got her nine names from which she got three calls and invitations for two dates that never materialized. From further questions it appeared that both appointments were made by one man who vanished with cold feet into the telephone.

Fifteen dollars was for one batch only. Second time around, rates were the same—profitable for the agency—but no satisfaction for Sally on lonely Saturday nights.

Ann's divorce was traumatic. Although she constantly needled her frustrating husband, she was totally unprepared for his departure. Even after the divorce she was not resigned to the separation. So three months later when he came to see the children with a lady on his arm, Annie was undone.

She was recommended to "Comfort . . . Computer for the Discriminating." Wallowing in self-pity, Annie's reason was upset by tears and fears. No penny-ante fifteen-dollar deal, this enterprise toadied to lonely people with money. They fronted their care and feeding station with paneled walls and chinoiserie, and deeply cushioned chairs. The client was easily clinched with personalized attention from a special staff, along with IQ, personality, and perfect-partner tests.

Before the gathered information was programmed into their computer, the cash—four hundred dollars—had to be in hand—*theirs*. Annie, in the grip of despair and failure and fear, paid promptly.

For this lump sum she was to receive a minimum of one name every other month for five years. (The theory was that only well-heeled ladies and gentlemen would readily spend so much to meet a mate, and delighted dates would then spin away in mutually splashy splendor.)

"Comfort" kept their word. Every other month Annie gets her list. She has three years to go under the agreement. But never has one of the prospects called her on the phone, and never has she had a date because of "Comfort."

Ann is pretty and able; her reason has returned, and she is glad her husband is gone. The only thing she would like back is her four hundred dollars, but she avers that this is a small price to pay for sanity.

So then, unless you want a robot (cousin to a computer), it's better to try for bachelors from natural births than to mess around with mechanical derivations.

But there is always the exception that doesn't prove the rule. Lenore for example.

Lenore was twenty-four and obese. She never had a date. Her fifty extra pounds put off even the most tolerant suitors, or the most dedicated sons of friends of the family. Lonely and fat is sadder than lonely and slim.

Unable to cope with her fudge-filled days, Lenore sent ten dollars to computer "Sure." She got six names. Four called. Two braved the width and breadth of "Sure's" stated specs and took Lenore to dine. One man named Clarence fell in love with her. To her 5'8" he was 6'5"; to her two hundred pounds he was three hundred. In the car he took the front and she the back.

Upshot of their overplump passion was a very large wedding. Then the joyous couple flew away to Alaska (where blubber is still in great demand) and where they live happily even now.

Not a fable but a true story that chalks one up for computers.

If you are a small gambler, you can try for ten or fifteen bucks. But even if you're sad, eccentric, and wealthy, don't invest in diamond-studded marriage machines. The law of averages will probably turn up more prospects anyhow.

Nothing is always bad or never good, and there *is* danger in every deviation. Meeting strangers through a mailbox or machine calls for caution, and other ways are better. The beautiful people are not likely to be in the classified anyway, and rarely are they found with application forms. But there is a sometimes for everyone, and every trail blazer has to try before he triumphs.

You Can't Go Home Again — Right Away

After you've leaped across a number of disappointing laps, the marriage you left behind may begin to look better. Wedded miseries are quite forgotten and only pleasant moments fill your memory.

If your ex has not yet flipped over anyone else, he may be backtracking also. And in that wishful recall of happier days, either or both of you might pick up the phone to call.

His familiar voice could end your vacillation quickly, one way or the other, with, "Let's have a drink and talk." And that reunion could be just a reaffirmation of old woes, or more happily, the building of a new start by lonely wanderers.

But remember that it takes a year to feel divorced. The decree is just a piece of paper, *fait accompli* in fact only. Severed ties exchange one trauma for another, and loneliness is an unleavened road.

It took you a long time to emerge in freedom. Give yourself a chance to cultivate detachment.

When is a safe time to see old spouses?

For some, right away. The marriage was a mistake for both, but they parted friends. Usually forceful and sensible souls, the break for them does not precipitate gloom.

Leaners who have bent their last reserve strength to bring about a permanent dissolution should stay away from former mates. Take the new and let old problems go; tears will lessen and the future lighten.

For most, ex-husbands are anathema. Such reunions provoke yesterday's irritations, and even temporary togetherness revives old problems.

It's better to bury old bones than to throw him one occasionally.

Most re-alliances come from loneliness and habit. That disagreeable but warm body that used to lie next to yours on cold nights seems more desirable in retrospect. Especially after endless nights of nothing but the tube and time.

Maybe you and former hubby can buck those headwinds better now, but don't be surprised to fall right back into the same unresolved problems and hangups.

Give it a cooling out period. A year. After the new you feels secure though single, then you can reencounter the castaway.

Every year in the United States some ten thousand couples who have suffered through divorce get married again—to each other. Dr. Paul Popenoe, advisor for the *Ladies Home Journal* series "Can This Marriage Be Saved?" hunted down two hundred of these twice-wed couples. A fourth of this number he found unhappy once more, a fourth uncertain and half cautiously content.

It also becomes evident by the similarity of second mates to original selections that hunters usually gravitate to similar personalities. The very characteristic that killed domestic tranquility initially may prepare the way for another wedding.

Wait—wait—wait.

Angela didn't. The day after the final decree was handed down she phoned Mike. He wasn't interested and what's more he was booked for a month.

She brooded while he flourished, and then one night she knocked on his door. The reconciliation was beautiful. Sexually they still swung like Gangbusters, but there was no communication on their feet. Neither missed the meeting of the minds however, and three days later they were respliced in a violent display of devotion.

And almost immediately both wished once more to be unwed.

Dolly didn't miss Matt at all. She adjusted to the great divide in a matter of months and was soon the fabled gay divorcée. Matt met her at a party where she was belle-ing the ball. Reenchanted with her charming smile and recollectable curves, he never left her side.

Through an alcoholic haze they got gushy about days gone by and left the party together.

He was the premarital Matt she remembered, and Dolly was a delight renewed to Matt.

Almost a year had elapsed since their split and both had mellowed.

They were married for ten years, divorced for two, and remarried for four when we talked. The second marriage couldn't be better, and now they are very secure.

The first time, Dolly said, was too soon and too fast. They were both in college struggling to stretch not-enough dollars most of the time. With financial disaster always imminent and exhaustion for both routine, they really didn't have a chance.

Now money is no problem. There's time for sex, for fun, for genuine affection.

As with any other miracle, a second-time wedding to a first-time failure requires determination, maturity, and luck for both bride and groom.

With some enough of a spark remains for renewal of former vows. But until the outside world proves weakness doesn't end at home, and that no one is perfect, reunion is a waste. When careful consideration over a period reveals real virtues in a discarded mate, then an old touch may mean a new attachment. Especially if the divided have children and china in common.

Post-divorce panic appears to be the same for most—male or female. Freedom launches a frantic search. Today with one out of four marriages coming unglued, the carnal encounter of re-licensed lovers is prodigious.

Along with falling panties, tears come on like flash floods of emotion.

Depression is a common factor in the post-partum period, again for both sexes. Highs and lows are extreme, and emotional thermometers dip or rise with sexual success or failure.

After about six months, emotions tend to level out. Both sexes cool off, regroup, and cease to grab whoever's closest. The virtue of quality takes precedence once more.

That's when the lady says "yes" to the brilliant broker, even though he's three inches shorter than she is. Or when tired Charlie gives away his little black book and settles down with understanding Evelyn. At last he prefers the quiet but fulfilling life to jet set glamour.

During rehabilitation, *don't return to the past.* When healing is accomplished you can reopen that book. Until you've traveled a little (from bed to bed?) you can't evaluate what victory lies in a repeated liaison.

If your loathing led as far as the courts, your caution should be extreme. Your ex's habits haven't changed. If he spoiled your moments of pleasure with nettles and puns, he will again. And if your nagging unsettled him before, you can bet your trusty trust fund his forbearance hasn't grown.

Before you take to his Peugeot, recall those unhappy days once more. Remember how he was always late, how he dawdled in the john, how he played poker till three (A.M.) and forgot to call?

How he ate, how he talked, how he chewed, how he walked? Didn't he say you couldn't dance? Didn't he grit his teeth or explode when you spent a few dollars for clothes?

But after you've fuddled with jerks and freaks and find your dreams still dreams, well, maybe then you can call, or listen to a reaffirmation of love.

And maybe—someday—you *can* go home again after all.

Duds for Divorcées

The clothes in your closet may not suit your new maneuvers. Okay for the easy living of a suburban housewife, those shirts and skirts are not the clothes you really need now.

Maybe as a matron you acquired cocktail dresses by the dozen, but quantity will never take the place of that special look singles sport today.

On the other hand, the hallmark of mediocrity is to follow the pack. As a single (again) girl, try to project a special image. Build your new wardrobe with a bold and exciting look.

Real females aren't mannikins.

The frozen perfection in fashion windows comes to life only on an elegant lady. But like plastic models, the perfect version of a heavenly vision happens only when the look swings from head to toe. What's more, your hair, face, body, and clothes need regular regrooming, separately, and then altogether. Somehow last year's Yves St. Laurent just doesn't look like today's.

After you've waded through most of those difficult personal problems, it's time to weed through your closet.

Be resolute.

Yes, it's hard to phase out old friends. But it's worse to riffle through the same old togs each day.

You'll never miss them once they're gone.

Don't keep the discards in the foyer. Call Goodwill (remember tax deductions) or put them out with the rubbish.

They won't go to waste. One of the handymen will salvage them for some less fortunate lady. And if they hang around the house, they'll soon be hanging once more on you, as conscience replaces valor.

Plan . . .

Once you have room for replacements, make a master plan. This is no time for rushing to the nearest clearance sale. Make a list. Itemize by category what you've kept. Then think before you decide on your needs.

If you're now a working girl your lists will overlap, since "after five" often runs to ten and past.

OCCASION	TYPE	SHOES, BAG	HOSE
Office (try for wash & wear pants suits, dresses, jumpers, etc.)	smart, plain (6)	mix or match basic shades best	beige brown black navy white
Office and on	expensive (4) jacket dresses— bare beneath?	maybe to match	

| *Formals*
As necessary | fine, sharp (1) | match,
blend | silver
gold
match
blend |
| *Weekend*
soirees | one outstanding
skirt with long
slit, halters (2)
shirts (2) | boots
anklestraps
platforms | definitely
nude to
the waist,
bare to
the toes |

OCCASION	COLOR
Sports	
Match for occasional play	white for tennis or yachts pastel for driving and walks
Nightwear	
Bet on a beautiful boudoir bouquet	black, blue, pink, or red white for marriage only
Undies	
Fresh, fragile dotted and dipped	matching sets sensashe!

NOTE: Underwear is wonderwear. No matter how demure above, daring is the word below!

Professional Shopping

Start with limited additions.

Collect your happy hunting gowns with care. One tip for shoppers who avoid devastating duds when they don't need them: If you run across a superb costume don't leave it for later. An occasion to fit an off-season find is certain to show up, and you'll be damning yourself if you didn't buy back when.

In the fitting room only you really know what suits your needs for now and then. The sales clerk can help with high-fashion hints, but don't expect her to overhaul your hull. She'll try. Still you must buy, and if the look doesn't gel for you it won't sell anyone else. If you're careful about what you pick, you'll always prize what you own.

There's a length that suits your figure, too. Don't be sold on longuettes by the tyranny of couturiers.

And if the mini looks like madness, too, just go for in between. The designers' dilemma gives you the choice.

Fickle fashion toys with other loves the very day she launches a new look. A monthly guide helps to grasp her varied moods.

Try *Women's Wear Daily* (leads the a la mode mags with advice on daily *couture*), or subscribe to one of the ladies fashion mags. Along with current styles, the contemporary scene is reviewed from a slick female viewpoint. Great skimming for hurried shoppers.

Cull your fashion hocus from the catechism of these journals. Be creative on *their* time.

Learn to recognize look-alikes that are half the price of their magazine super models. And pay attention to boutique offerings. Trimmings can initiate a whole new style, add class to more than basic black.

Wow!

Married, you dressed for neighbors, for ladies of the Saturday night set, and for committee meetings. Competition was a "can you top this" for females only.

Clothes do make the man, you know! *Your* clothes, that is.

Gentlemen today strut and preen in their own sartorial splendor. And they want their women to match their suddenly glorious look. Conservative colors and cuts for the male have given way to bold sport jackets, loud shirts, and bell bottom trousers. Can the lady wear less?

So now you must dress for guys. *Guys*. And since there isn't enough manpower to satisfy all the gals, you've got to more than meet the competition.

Be a *provocateur*.

Learn the tricks of the trapper.

How? Here's a little how.

Example: A sensational baring of the breast is not nearly as effective as daring cleavage where an any minute pop up looks possible.

Example: hot pants showing slender legs are nice, but not nearly as seductive as limbs beneath a slashed-to-the-waist, long, long skirt. Just watch the reaction when you cross your legs!

What he can't quite spy is what he can't quite forget. You can really unhinge old Bill with the half-off scene. The message: mystery—that slightly open door.

Note: This advice does not apply to office hours. From nine to five stay buttoned up and Peter Panned. The great white-paper daddy won't appreciate undulating derrieres or unrestrained breastworks (not in his office anyway). Use your sexy armor after six and away from business associates.

The jacket dress solves such problems. Wear it behind your desk and be demure. Then unzip at the Zigzag Lounge and flash the waiting décolletage. Weekends are for WOW. Go braless, unstockinged, midriff bare, or backless. You can't be too brazen because peek-a-boo is the name of the game. Your date *might* show amazement at your daring, but will register delight *for sure*. Teasing surpasses total revelation, but neat measurements are necessities for deliberate provocation.

Anyway, by now you've either got the idea or not, and will or won't follow through with research on what looks and works the best almost on or almost off your most appealing parts.

The possibilities are worth a little thoughtful planning.

Safety Factor — A Friend

Everybody needs an ear, and hurts heal fastest with tender loving care.

Pour it out to a friend.

When a guilty conscience churns unheard, the psyche is in trouble.

Recriminations are just a form of repeated self-punishment. A friend can help you over the hurdles with friendly understanding. And she can get the same comfort from you.

Suppose you take up with a married man. Morning after misery gets you down. Last night's romantic bells ding a different dong. All of you is sorry. He isn't yours, he won't be back, and now you're just a notch on another belt.

Tell your friend. Real friends unravel twisted rigging and help you back to self-respect, which is what it's all about.

One friend. One confidante. One lady who really counts. That's all it takes.

She listens and reassures, but it's the sound of your own sorry voice that pacifies your troubled soul.

She could be a he. Occasionally a man and woman weave platonic ties that bind. But usually the patting turns to petting, and final soothing is in the sack.

Though women are wary of women, they can be loyal and supportive buddies. And you won't need a psychiatrist to couch your conscience at fifty bucks a session if you can find a friend.

How to have a friend:

1. Be loyal.

   a. If you promise not to tell, don't. Gossips are gum-dums.

   b. Don't take an overactive interest in her beaux. Her favorites are off limits for little old you.

   c. Send chicken soup when she's ill. It's nice to know somebody out there is thinking, even if it's just about soup.

   d. If she's desolate, call off your date. A friend in need nets a friend in need.

2. Help is a half a dozen.

   a. If her hair looks unattractive, say so. Help can be courageous criticism.

   b. Include her in on happy accidents. If your guy has a friend, and she's fresh out, work her in.

3. Remember:

   a. Her birthday.

b. Her Mother's name.

c. How smart her children are.

d. How much time she spends with you on the telephone.

And lots more—mutual concern and consideration.

A serious, sincere, understanding friend is the best safety valve that you can have. Seek and you shall find. Care and you will keep.

Diet, Anyone?

Demand for excess blubber isn't much anymore. But if the fashion for fat ever reignites, present supply will be more than sufficient.

Fatties are unfulfilled, insecure, and flatulent.

The question is: Which comes first, the problem or the fat?

Overeating is compulsive. And smoking, if you're still lighting cigarettes to diminish your appetite, doesn't always abate the belly-god. Seeking a substitute for love, sex, or recognition, 34 million overweight Americans guzzle, gobble, and swallow their way into Fatsburg.

Chewing chases the blues. Temporarily.

Overindulgence in dumplings is just another kind of suicide. Insurance statistics point out that:

1. Overweights are never winners on the risk sheet.

2. High blood pressure is more common in the hefty.

3. Arthritis and diabetes are more frequent in the fat.

4. Strokes and disorders of the heart tend to attack the corpulent . . .

5. Hardening of the arteries is common in the weighty.

Excess weight strains organs and muscles, stretches skin to fit the bulging fat beneath.

For searching singles a little flab can mean a lot—varicose veins, fallen arches, bulging belly. And when hips and thighs outflank normal fluctuation, there goes the ball game!

No love survives the persistence of spreading rumps and lapping rolls stuffed into garroting girdles.

Mrs. William Paley, very beautiful, very rich, and very thin, once told a journalist that a lady can never be too beautiful, too rich, or too thin.

So now you know what you knew all along— you mustn't gain an ounce. And if you have a pound that doesn't belong, it's got to go.

Okay . . . How Do I?

Diets of medical merit are available from your doctor and should be followed only with his advice. Reducing fads make the scene in magazines weekly, and almost every paper carries a daily diet hint or two (most effective fillers) .

But there are no magic formulas.

To cast off extra avoirdupois you must eliminate extra calories. It's so simple it's silly.

Starving is too extreme. You can't do that for long, and only under strict medical supervision.

The water method works for some. Pounds just float away with the liquid drain. Eight glasses of water a day slosh down lean beef, fish, eggs, cottage cheese, chicken, and turkey. No other food allowed. Alcohol is off limits.

This diet calls for regular sorties to the john where panties rise and fall with faucet-failure frequency. To facilitate the waterworks, sign on temporarily as purser of a powder room. That way you can gain while you are losing!

Water pills squeeze out a pound or so, for a temporary loss only. Though some women retain fluids to the point of puffiness, most control edema with sensible restriction of salt. But just before menstruation, diuretics really help, and some doctors recommend their use.

Diet pills are always in demand, but physicians dispense them with care. Part of the "speed" scene, they may increase your blood pressure and heart rate or charge you up for sleepless nights. Continued use diminishes their deterrent effect on appetite and can also lead to addiction. Like cigarettes, they don't deter an inveterate cheater.

Skipping a meal doesn't really cut calories either. You'll probably eat more at the next meal.

Medical sources aver that there is no scientific proof for the magical properties of unsweetened grapefruit juice or grapefruit itself. But dieters have subtracted from their thickness with grapefruit preceding every meal, because *belief is half the battle*. And that brings me to my super shed suggestions for the weight-conscious divorcée.

Not scientific or medical in origin, not advertised, recognized, or touted by the de-tonated, they represent twenty years of watching weight (mine) and how and where it went (the quickest).

Think thin.

Full power of the mind is unprobed, and its limits undetermined. When human mental power is completely developed, perhaps we'll be able to tan our hides by tuning our heads, or propel our disembodied selves through the ozone on soaring mentally motivated flights.

Whatever the mind can perceive is possible.

And sometimes you can hook onto a very powerful wavelength.

I did.

I began to *think thin*.

Ten pounds was my extra avoirdupois. And I lost it by *thinking thin*.

Whether this mental approach will work for you I do not know. But if your yearned-for loss is small, it's worth a try. And even if you're bursting with obesity these simple mental gymnastics might correspond with the doctor's more scientific restraints. At any rate, they can't hurt.

Think Thin

In the privacy of your bedroom check yourself for
surplus weight. Look at the naked you with honest
objectivity. Then try for the old dab of flab. If
your fingers can fold more than one inch of flesh
at waist, rib cage, or thigh, you are overweight.

And you ought to *think thin*.

Stand before a full-length mirror. Rivet your
gaze to your reflected measurements. *Concentrate*.
Bend those mental beams to your desired deline-
ations. Contemplate two figures. One real, the
other imagined but clear. Two of you. What is
and what will be. Then fade the double image to
one, the favored form—5-10-15 kilos cast away.

Hold that concentration. Freeze. Force a feeling of weight slipping away. Your mind will reach
to reject unwanted hunks of chunk.

Don't move. Try to hold the sensation of refitted

flesh and skin. Mental intensity should tighten every muscle. Then relax. Properly executed, the process can't last more than three minutes to start. Each succeeding effort (with deeper concentration) will stretch your strings, physical and mental, a little more.

Truly mind over (corporeal) matter.

Think thin before you go to sleep. You'll be skinnier with the dawn.

Don't eat after you *think thin*.

Don't plan a specific diet.

Before meals *think thin*. And your mind will outmaneuver mastication.

After a few days *thinking thin* becomes a habit. Lying in the sun, typing at the IBM, walking on the beach, *thinking thin* will be your thing.

And you will begin to be thin. Or thinner.

It's worth a try, and it can't hurt. If calories don't count and intellect activates, you're on your way.

Then there's another favorite theory, perhaps a phallusy—but helpful to uninhibited heavies.

Losing Weight While Making Love

Try it.

Weigh in before the marvelous whirl. Check the scale before you get under the sheets. Whatever mark you make on Detecto before will drop when it's all over. The longer the lower.

An outrageous scheme for reducing? Wrong. A wonderful method for making minus with a plugged in plus.

I kid you not. But—there is a but. You have to enjoy. If his touch intoxicates; if his fingers enflame your fevered skin; if you tingle, if you shudder, if you shake, calories will burn up twice as fast in your body. When the scene is ended, when the frenzy fades, love will leave you lighter.

Medical support is missing here, but again, it's worth a try. Find a scale and a passionate man; get weighed before and after.

Perhaps the possibility of losing pounds will pique desire.

What a dilly of a diet! What a way to conquer fat!

Why Worry?

Another great way to make pounds melt is to worry. And not just about problems that matter. Whoppers deserve a little worry. In fact, real distress often stimulates appetite and fretting in earnest adds fat.

The best way to slenderize is to worry about a man. Senseless worry is cheap, convenient, and quick. There is always a man to worry about, no special equipment is required, and it maintains your readiness for any trivial problem.

What to fret about is not important.

Any old disport in a storm.

If he doesn't call promptly at eight, frown.

If he doesn't call at eight-thirty, pace.

By nine, if he hasn't buzzed, burn.

At nine-thirty, you've waited long enough. Worry!

If you fret from ten to twelve with absolutely no snacking in between, you will scald away an ounce or two.

He says he cares, vows his everlasting love. You succumb to his insistent passion; sex is super, and you cling like ivy up the eaves. All is well when he heads for home. Your erotic romp has popped a pound or so. Go for more. Worry! Did he declare his love just to get you in the sack? Wonder! Will his passion wane by dawn's baring light? Worry! Will he return to your bed again, or was this spree the whole durn thing? Worry! Again a word of caution to the successful worrier. Don't eat between pouts and sighs. By morning you'll probably be minus three pounds or more.

Marvelous, fabulous worry. Be sure to keep it up.

If he should interrupt your fury by calling at dawn to plan another rendezvous, don't worry! You can worry again when he waves goodbye once more.

If thinking thin helps to hound the pounds, and super sack scenes dissolve your fat, try a combination. Immediate results are known to have come from the following physio-diet therapy.

Be sure to check with your doctor first. He may want to lose a little too.

1. Choose a diet you can share. The water-protein scheme is simple. Not much cooking, few supplies. Let him pay for the steaks, chicken, chops, lobster, crab meat, cottage cheese, and fish. You can supply the eggs and water.

On second thought he can buy the eggs, too.

2. Choose a man you can share the diet with. For assured success invite a virile friend—overweight *and* oversexed.

3. Take a vacation or be sick for a few days. Stock the frig and check the water pipes.

All set? Start Sunday night. Weigh in and think thin.

Once he understands the strategy you can TT (Think Thin) together. Three minutes is all that mental effort takes; then watch your corpulence disappear!

Locked in for a week with only love and protein, both of you will start the slimward slide with ecstasy and cottage cheese.

You probably won't want to advertise your unorthodox and watery week of losing weight. But you can think about it when you're thinking thin alone again, and those belly flutters will help to restrain regain.

Sports Section

You'll find that weight won't melt away like wax. No matter how helpful thinking thin may be, or how carefully you decalorize, your curves require constant watching. Skinny or fat, everyone should exercise.

No matter how tired you feel before muscular activity, your body will shift into high as blood courses more rapidly around its familiar path. And when worrying or anxiety tire you from head to toe, try exercise instead of a nap. A ten-minute workout will turn you on again.

Of course there are ways to offset the boredom of solitary exercise. Like other health programs, exercise is more fun in pairs. Just remember that however you practice your dozen, the routine must be daily.

If you decide to include physical education

with your duo-diet program, your guy might be swayed by special bedroom activities. With tandem situps, pushups, and stretching, he may even decide to be the leader. After all, fun and games beat drinks at the bar on a sunny afternoon. At least you'll have a reason to race your motor.

New Slants for Slimmers

1. Chinups for two are really intimate. Be sure the chinning bar is fastened tight to the door jamb. Sudden collapse could postpone *all* athletic efforts. You take one side, baby the other. Rub his nose when you rest your chin.

2. A bicycle built for two is fun. If you ride around town be sure to let him drive and don't be a back-seat cycler. To argue you must stop and so defeat the purpose. Bike-sighting around the city on a quiet Sunday is great for hangovers and haunches. For stay-at-homes, built-in wheels are out, too crowded for double duty.

3. If you have a pool, splash off together. Swimming any style will keep your chassis lean. Underwater capers have been tried with some success. But, unless you're a champ in the water, leave snorkel passes and scuba antics to the experts who

know what to try for when they dive.

4. Jogging is great. Follow the rules for steady results. Nice way to meet new people, too. Bernice was a jogger. She ran around the park each evening after work. Len was a runner, too. They passed each other daily, smiled, and finally ran the track together. He asked her for a date. Over cokes they discussed the virtues of aerobics. That was in May. In June they made an indoor dash; now they're jogging jointly in his pad—muscled, married, and wildly in love.

5. Yoga has possibilities, too. Viola liked to stand on her head—part of her daily routine. Upsidedown she dreamed of finding the perfect mate. One day an athletic widower sauntered into her life. When she convinced him that bottoms up is better, he programmed some innovations on ordinary yoga. Now their thing is much too complicated to ever teach another. Body sweat switched a lark to love, and Viola doesn't dream anymore.

6. Remember how to play Tag? A marvelous way to warm a winter night. And when just two are in the game, chills get chased (and the chaste get chills). Duck, dip, somersault, slide, and run. If your fella thrives on the thrill of pursuit, he'll appreciate your ingenuity.

7. Do you have a sauna? Great! Gymnastics followed by heat help the muscle-bound. Be careful though. Don't burn your suitor. Yes, you want him heated through, but not scorched. If, like most ladies, you have no deep-heat lounge, don't despair. A shower will recondition your skipper.

Lather him while he soaps you down. Clean and close in water that's gentle and warm never fails to stretch the illusion of love.

8. Of course the bed is the place to battle the bulge. For situps and pushups, the mattress can't be beat. If you're not too carried away count to twenty. By that time you ought to be carried away or forget it.

Real gymnastics just won't work in the boudoir drill. Again you've got to be creative. But—before you undertake this strenuous route for lovers, take a first-aid refresher.

If baby's muscles are middle-aged, he might be out of shape. First Olympic efforts might do him in, so you ought to know how to revive your recruit with mouth to mouth resuscitation (certified method for young sweet things to save their rich but aging Don Juans).

Well then, now you know. Two can depound better than one, and you're bound to work harder if they're *his* toes you're trying to touch.

Consider a triple header—*thinking thin, double diet,* and *exercise for two.* The schedule sounds tough, but results could be astounding!

Never let measurements get out of bounds. Not even an eighth of a dab of flab.

Even if you hover between lovers, stay ahead of the gain.

Just do your own things.

Everyone should specialize in a sport anyway.

More Pointers For Peppy People

9. Cabana clubs are first-rate for staying trim *and* socializing. So get in the swim for summer. Same for tennis. Racket clubs are also meeting places where he and she can play a set and make a set all in the same afternoon.

10. Golf? Marvelous! If you walk. Walking is great! You'll feel revitalized after that eighteen-hole hike. But if you use a cart, forget it. It takes more calories to damn your dubs than to steer that convenient grassmobile.

11. Unless you resort to rowing or have to bail, don't count on boats for exercise. The motor and water do the work. Most of the time the only part you move is your elbow (in spurts, with spirits).

12. In the end, routine is what does it. Elly knows that. When she was twenty-five, old age seemed hardly a skip away. She started a routine of exercise for winter, plus a spring and summer regimen. Pushups, situps, solo and thigh exercises were just part of her daily pattern. Elly played tennis, rode, jogged, and swam.

She stuck to her vigorous regimen. Three days a week, no matter what, she exercised.

Now, at thirty-five, her breasts are hard and high, her arms smooth and firm, her legs long and lovely. Elly's face is fresh and full of happy smiles. She looks ten years younger than she is. What's more, she feels it too.

Perseverance pays.

And . . . the key word is *constant*.

Yoga, calisthenics, tennis, swimming, riding a bike, making love—all great for the figure.

But unless you're the gal that plays the game, another will make the score.

Stay Thin Thoughts That Everyone Needs and Ought to Know But Doesn't

Mother Nature spreads a great variety of edibles on her table. She meant for us to balance our nutrient intake. Don't leave your selection to chance. Proper nutrients help you to ward off disease and stay young.

Eat a variety of foods.

Devotees of dietetics stress the need for proper nourishment. And health nuts push organic nutrition.

Although science is more sophisticated in its recent calculation of human needs, most of the "Do eats" differ little from what we learned in health and hygiene classes long ago. Complete protein foods assure growth and repair of body cells. They keep your skin smooth and soft and provide zest for living in your vital, energetic, and unvirtuous new life.

Protein isn't an aphrodisiac. Oysters, contrary to an old wives tale, contribute no more to bacchanalia than other proteins. But without at least eighty to one hundred grams of protein each day, your diet is deficient and it may affect your sex life.

Don't fast when your body needs food. Eat enough to satisfy but not to glut. Lettuce is just as good with lemon as drowned in mayonnaise. You can learn to like the lean side of life.

Be practical. Be prudent. Make healthy eating an everyday habit.

Teach yourself to dine judiciously; think thin, and consider not only your conformation but to whom it might conform.

Detailed diets are available from your physician and every life insurance company. If you're a devotee of forms, by all means decorate your walls with "what to do's." But don't forget the dual-diet delight.

You can't blame avoirdupois on corpulent or paunchy relatives. What you eat is what you are —and where there's a will there's no (over) weight.

Beauty and the Best

Youth is the Yum Yum tree; beauty the bonus in the candy box.

And the face of fortune is sexy but subtle.

Most ladies who wish to be lovely are *lazy*.

Your countenance deserves special attention. It's your face. And no one wants a winner more than the wearer.

Professionals can teach you how to apply the paint, but your particular nuances are for you to find.

To achieve a personal razzle dazzle you'll have to experiment; gather samples, kinds, colors, co-ordinates, and try them out.

Most cosmetic houses have samplers. If you con the clerk just a bit she'll reach beneath the counter. Nobody wants to look like Halloween, but bagging be-gorgeous goodies for a "try it yourself" at home is a dandy trick. You really earn some treats when you take the time to know your face.

Nobody exactly fits the norm, which nobody can define anyway. You've been facing your phiz for years and ought to know what's normal for you. The cosmetician won't catch your act but once, but will know how to add the little extras that make the *big* difference. Take the program she proposes, then add and subtract to reface your own surface.

Basic for any beauty you may have is clean skin. Most women select cleansing cream, but if your face loves the faucet feel, try a pharmaceutical soap. The rest of you will enjoy this soft touch, too. Basis (Duke Laboratories) is pure, lasts forever, and a favorite of dermatologists. If you still get a hickey now and then, Fostex and Phisohex are surgical soaps that wipe bacteria clear off the map (yours, that is), but prescriptions are necessary.

Moisturizers add a dewy look and feel. Use from forehead to chest; chance won't work on the wrinkles in your neck, so you should. Treat a wrinkled crevice with moisturizer and watch the lotion go to work.

Save pennies from martinis at midday and keep your cream closet full instead. Proper provision for the skin they love to touch will keep the male-men buying your martinis anyway.

Examine your skin. The color varies slightly, doesn't it? Foundations—cream, liquid, or lotion —can bring up your bloom or mask a muddy tone. Try one tint for daytime's revealing light, another for evening's softer shades. Powder is a sometime friend. A lot makes paste; a little keeps makeup Swan Lake smooth.

You are the swami. And you've got to experiment to know what's best for you. Your makeup can be cakey, flakey, or super soft. "Just right" for your skin could be all wrong for your councilor. Try before you buy.

Perfect is the name, and all day is the game.

Sometimes there isn't a "just right" shade in the kind of makeup you like—so buy two and mix a master. It's a little tricky to combine exactly the right amount time after time, but this soon gets to be habit. Like your favorite recipe (a dash of salt, a dip of butter, a touch of dill!) practice brings it all together.

Make the most of what you have.

Dazzling eyes attract the male more than topless waitresses or dancers. Not enough is overlooked, but too much eye makeup can make you look like a zombie. You're the artist and the jury.

If you are over thirty, water shadows are best. They fill in little wrinkles on the lid and lie smooth even under powder. Dry shadows lump in lines (except on youthful skin) and smudge where deposits are deeper.

Match the color of your eyes, not your dress or personality: Brown or hazel orbs seem larger, warmer with shades of cinnamon and gray. Surrounded by azure, blue eyes balloon. Use lavender on violet; shades of green over green eyes. Cosmetic clerks are urged to sell the rainbow, but you only need one pot of gold.

A darker tone is meant for the crease between brow and eye. Gray or brown is always okay here, with white or tints of white on the bone beneath the brow.

Don't darken eyebrows. Unless they are haphazard and sparse, leave them alone. The natural look is best with removal of wandering hairs only. Line from corner of the eye to outside end of brow should be a forty-five degree angle; trim if it goes beyond.

Again, the configuration of your brow should fit your face.

Before you shorten, paint out the part to be removed. If it fits, fine; if not, "touch not a hair."

False eyelashes are terrific. If your own lashes are beautiful, another pair on top is most effective. Frustrating initially to attach yourself, practice does make perfect. Again, find a system that suits you. Necessary tools are simple—toothpicks and surgical glue (any good drugstore). Wear medium-length lashes locked into your own with a gently poking toothpick.

Your lashes should start about one eighth of an inch from the inside of the eye and extend to the outer edge. If they are too long, clip the outer side—*never* the part that approaches the nose. To trim lash length use a single-edge razor on a very flat surface.

Lower-lid lashes are not necessary to make you look like a million, but sometimes they are fun too. To increase the length of your own, powder, then stroke mascara, powder again, and mascara once more.

Liner on the lower eyelid should be lighter than what you use above. If you like, shadow can be brought around and under the eye before mascara and liner—thicker at the outer edge and dwindling to the inside corner, blended and very subtle.

Remember that eyelashes are not only for special occasions. Accustom yourself to daily attachment or forget the whole thing.

In fashioning your new face, like acquiring a new wardrobe for your new status, never forget you create an image—a pace-setter model for a more assured, purposeful you.

Now, how about rouge? Cheek shading has changed in name and texture, but the idea's the same. Blusher, bronzer, or gel—each resurrects natural roses of yesteryear.

Powder should be applied before lashes inlaid, unless you use a rubber puff and pat. Otherwise lashes are flecked with white. Translucent powder suits all purposes. Use a dampened cotton ball, or covered ice cube to set.

Whether lip color comes from a tube or pot, for better bind, powder lips first. A yellow toner under lipstick will keep the color true.

Be sure to clue lip color to what you are wearing, and please note: if you let your "eyes have it" keep your lipstick on the light side. Pale and luminous glosses have a kissable look.

We've discussed hair above, so just a reminder

here. Keep it well-kempt, silky, and shaped. Guys sometimes dig a girl from the rear if her hair is shining and clean. And if the bow matches the stern, it's full speed ahead for the crew.

Night creams do a lot. When you find one that doesn't mess up the pillow or the fellow, try regular use for lasting results.

The face that gets my vote changes little from daylight to dark. Just the shadow should be subdued by day. This face can get you to work, appear at a lunch, or keep you glamorous through dinner.

Get beautiful baby—it's the biggest asset in your bong-bong box.

Swingers — How to Be
Tarzan and Jane Without a Rope

Since when is sex a team sport?

Since swinging, that's when!

Swinging, a new kind of sharing, where husbands and wives, boyfriends and girlfriends band together in groups in a constant search for variety on the sex scene.

For the sensuous single it might or might not be a sexational way to increase exposure.

If you are overinhibited or squeamish, forget it. The format is probably too *avant-garde*. But if sexual abandon is buttoned into your survival kit, you could become an accomplished swinger.

Swingers' magazines are intended for the sexually oriented, serving as contact and catalyst for people to meet and swing. The salacious slicks also feature clubs, legitimate organizations that accept couples and single women as members, but refuse men without partners.

Bulging at the sexy seams, these gamic gazettes feature erotic photographs and advertisements from subscribers (swingers searching for new swingers) from all over the U.S. and abroad.

About two million swingers are supposed to favor this incendiary idea of mate-swapping. Gilbert Bartell *(Group Sex)*, in tracking the country's swinger population, found more than eight thousand practicing members in Chicago, while a *Time* interviewer reported four thousand followers in Atlanta. The Editor of *Swinger's Choice* puts Miami's burgeoning devotees at two thousand. So it's no surprise that aficionados support more than fifty sex-flavored journals of varying size, quality, and cost. Printed bimonthly, the better glossies are expensive, about three dollars a copy, fifteen dollars by the year.

Select (New Jersey) is the oldest and largest guide for swingers. *Swinger's Life* (Pennsylvania) and *Swinger's Choice* (Florida) are smaller but similar. Each follows an erotic pattern of presentation, filled with photographs of bosomy solicitors, uncovered crotches, and open enumerations of sexual preferences.

Sixty to seventy percent of the ladies swing either way. So if you adore sex and are slightly lesbian, you are certain to fit the swinging scene.

Ads are run by partners or singles. Designation is by a letter preceding box numbers: couples, *C*, Male, *M*, Female, *F*. Pictures are usually of the lady, although an occasional narcissistic male poses for posterity, covering his accouterments with hand or handkerchief.

Advertisers seek fun and games in a wide range of sexual diversity. Some distaffers specify girls or couples; some men seek other men; some draw a color line while others maintain that color is unimportant; some detail B/D (bondage and discipline) or S/M (Sadomasochism) ; some rule out perversion by stipulating straight swingers only; and neophytes beg forbearance and plead for patient teachers.

As page after page of erotica are revealed, the female form loses its divinity. If a portrait pleases a reader, he writes to the advertiser through the magazine, sending along fifty cents to a dollar plus loose postage for each letter. The swingers' code requires answer for answer. After this exchange, approach is on a personal level.

Get-togethers follow four distinct patterns. Socials are not unlike any other club meeting. Member and guest couples eat, drink, dance, and size each other up for future fornication. In the case of swingers it takes more than two to tango; both halves of both teams must agree or there will be no subsequent love scene.

A swinging party takes two different forms. At casual affairs members may remain dressed and indulge or not as they desire. But if the invitation so specifies, guests *must* disrobe at the door. Nude, they indicate a willingness for carnal encounters. Still, it's swinger's choice. Even unclothed the individual decides whether he (or she) wishes to participate or not.

Some swinging households feature wall-to-wall

mattresses where bodies tangle in a mass of arms and legs, heads and hands. For some, group grasping is repugnant. These closet swingers only lose their inhibitions in the bedroom, where two is a crowd (but three is better).

For swingers, switching means sharing.

Mates claim that shared sexual experiences deepen devotion and love, reinforce mutual dependence and trust, and improve their personal zest for sex.

Cheating is unpalatable to married swingers, who have their own unwritten laws. They do not take kindly to voyeurs or male homosexuals. The women are allowed to change, however, and that is why an extra girl is handy at the hoedown. (But even though over half the lady swingers switch, most prefer to make it with a man.)

Swingers protect each other and watch out for unescorted gals. They recognize the possibility of an occasional pervert in the woodpile and are always wary of strangers.

A surprising number of professionals—teachers, doctors, lawyers, dentists, even a smattering of young ministers, dig the swinging scene. And an unestimated number of satisfied single women who want sex but not marriage.

Emily is twenty-eight, a Vassar graduate, and a candidate for her Ph.D. in history. She swings once or twice a week with Warren who introduced her to the swapping syndrome over a year ago. At first she was reluctant, apprehensive. Now her eagerness surpasses his. "It's better than having a different car in my driveway every night," she laughs. "And it satisfies my need for new sexual encounters with no necessity for emotional involvement. And Warren looks after me. Protects me, sort of."

Does she love Warren? Maybe. There's no hurry to make that decision. Meanwhile she's met other men at swinging socials and parties who are possibilities for future relationships, if her feelings for Warren diminish.

"Moreover," Emily stresses, "I haven't swung with any of them. It's not that big a deal. Sex is just necessary and swinging makes it fun."

Swingers are serious about lasting friendships that spring from swing.

"It's really a fantastic way to meet great people," rhapsodized a married twenty-two-year-old teacher with a face like a fairy princess. "Everybody cares about everybody. We really make love not war." Maybe so. But swinging *isn't* for everybody.

In this environment the single (again) girl might broaden her taste and perfect her technique but end up with no emotional maturation and little chance of finding love. For the gal who wants to go steady only with herself it's perfect. But for the desolate woman who wants a permanent hand to hold, it's a difficult road. There are no extra men allowed, and most of the male partners aren't interested in a new liaison. Detached and cool, swingers cop out after the kicks. Couples go home together, but the extra girl leaves alone.

For women who dig calculated sex (fornicate and forget), the swinging scene might be the answer. Another out of the way place to meet a fella, perhaps, but not one of the better bastions for single men.

If you decide to try, good luck on the way-out, very sexy, swinging ladder for ladies.

Singles Clubs — How to Meet
the Losers and the Cruisers

Divorcées in great numbers attend singles clubs. Also widows and single singles. And sometimes a married single mixes in just for fun.

Quantity exceeds quality just as women are more plentiful than those they seek.

It's difficult to take a stand on this kind of mix and match. Opinions vary. There are those who feel that singles clubs provide a haven and a home for those that need it. Shy Sherrill won't meet smooth Dick at a wine-tasting party, but she might meet reticent Harry at a singles social. The chances are small that he will turn out to be her next spouse, but it could happen.

Every month bulletins from singles clubs list matriculations, one or more from Misses to Madams—marriages that grow out of club activities.

There are loads of satisfied members who

wouldn't miss a meeting—and who don't, year after year after year. Others, early in the divorce aftermath, visit one or two club functions and disappear, disgusted.

It's more fun to belong and hope than to sit by the fire and mope. At least you have a chance, and you might even get your choice.

Some of the groups have yearly dues ranging from five to twenty dollars. Most charge for mixers such as coffees, tea dances, house parties, and full-blown balls with sit-down dinners.

Main complaint from the women—the men are chintzy. "When the party's over," sigh disappointed gals, "the fellows won't even spring for a soda. They meet you at the dance after you pay your own way in, and they bug out way before the Burger King."

But the boys have a gripe or two themselves. Said a disgruntled ex-member, "The girls kept getting uglier and fatter. I couldn't meet anything but losers. I got tired telling them to get lost. Who needs it? The world is full of women!"

To give the club syndrome its true due, however, the happies must be singled out. Some of the clusters really pull together those who need mates and pair them up.

Try it. You might like it. You can't suffer much from a few exposures. Whatever else happens, you'll taste a little wine, sip a little punch, converse over coffee, and dance once or twice. If the stag you're searching for isn't there, you might meet a girl who knows another place to look.

And like the lady on the boat, or in the bar or the filling station, your lucky lad might just be making the singles scene on the same night that you are.

A word of caution to classified ad perusers. Unscrupulous organizers sometimes advertise through the newspapers for singles to join their clubs, ostensibly for the purpose of meeting members of the opposite sex. Actually, most of these come-ons are commercial. They want to give you dancing lessons, or charge large amounts for parties that put one and one together.

Be on the alert for those "con" vocations. And don't be taken in. Under the guidance of a talented teacher the mambo lessons go on forever while those single partners appear only periodically, if at all.

It's all part of the old con game of making money on other people's misery.

You can dance better at Parents Without Partners or its equivalent. Make sure you understand the objectives of a get-together group before you agree to pay. Don't part with any money until you're sure you'll receive *quid pro quo*. It's all right always—and not in the least embarrassing— to hesitate where money is concerned. And better before than after.

Laura called the "Rare Man" Singles Club, paid plenty for twenty dancing lessons, with partners to match. She got a few half-hearted two-steps and a lukewarm tumble from the tuba player. Club dances were a disaster with continued offers of hanky-panky she didn't want or need. The single men were rare all right—rarely there at all.

Sometimes a recommendation is needed to join a singles club of substance. And however dull the legitimate groups may be, they hope for miracles for their members, or at least happiness from their meetings.

Be sure the club you choose has a good reputation. You'll probably be proselytized to join by a friend anyway. Dance the frug, chat with the men, don't expect the jet set, and judge for yourself.

Conclusion

Conclusions are usually disasters.

Abrupt or long-drawn, they usually miss the point of summation.

What's good for one person may be ghastly for another. You, divorcée from the suburbs or small two-faced town, may like those brazen ladies who peck away at your changed status. Their barbs may be your cup of tea.

And if you prefer to sit tight in your cozy nest with familiar pictures and popcorn, good for you.

At least you know what you want. Or what you don't.

And just because the West has more brawn, that doesn't mean a mate won't turn up on the first tee of your local country club. It happens every now and then.

Just as a novice becomes a star, you might just be suddenly terrific—in everything.

Maybe you don't need a guide to have fun. Maybe no advice will help. You'll just resort to a rocking chair for comfort and squeaky consolation.

But there is a conclusion.

When the smoke clears and all façades are struck down, the conclusion demands to be heard. Only one answer echoes down the common hall and bounces from the dead-end wall—

Nobody wants to be alone.

Nobody really wants to be alone.

Beyond the need for sex, is just the need to touch; to watch a tennis match together on TV; to walk in rainy woods, hands clasped, hidden in an outsized pocket; to dine by candlelight, sipping draughts from sharing eyes; the need to love . . . the need to nest, to share sorrows and wonders, tears and laughter.

Divorce isn't the end of anything except mistakes. Divorce is a chance for another chance.

Because *nobody* wants to be alone.

The guy who didn't call you back will call another and another until he finds a winner. For *him*. So don't cry at his disappearance. He wouldn't have been the one for you.

But time in its motion, luck in its unpredictable way, will bring another for you. And another. Until you too find the right one.

Exceptions? Yes, of course. Disappointments, wrong choices, drop-outs, wash-outs, dullards— women who can't make up their minds, gals who balk at less than love's young dream. There are, indeed, carloads of losers.

And there are some, of course, who quit, who

don't want the woes of competition.

But the loners are fewer than the lonely.

Although the human race seems bent on multiplying itself to extinction, and physical closeness to strangers is an all-day way of life, still the spirit despairs of achieving that oneness of two that makes living worthwhile.

The search goes on. For women alone. For men alone. To find each other in the space that defines the length of life—from here to there.

The odds are that you will succeed. Your warmth and openness will meet with another's. Chemistry and a careful plan of action can work.

What if he has a groovy pad with paneled den and two inches of carpet to keep his feet warm? His needs are more basic than fluff under his toes. He needs a woman just as you need a man. And it's your mission to drive him bananas with that message. When the message is in one medium only, even holdouts relent and fall into line.

That special flicker in your ticker is a pretty good indicator. And when your tummy feels funny, too, you can be sure he's having a twinge or two himself. Have confidence. Love does happen now and then, and you won't strike out all the time.

How strange that women think men are never without a suitable companion, never, not even for a night. How equally odd that men picture the lady of their choice as besieged by legions of suitors far less vulnerable than themselves.

Meanwhile most guys and gals are scraping

around in the bottom of the lonely barrel for a little love, hoping desperately for a lot.

Tom is eighteen, in college. He lives on campus with ten thousand other T-shirted and jeaned students. They laugh, play rock 'n' roll records at full volume, rise like jumping jacks to catch a ball, and watch the world go by. Boys watch girls and girls watch boys.

And they wait.

In a bizarre show of indifference they search for emotional fulfillment.

Tom digs Hazel. Hazel digs Tom. Their eyes meet and communicate.

Loneliness is stilled for a day or a week or an hour with hands tenderly held, bare feet linked —leg on leg.

When Hazel finds another, Tom will have the gutty pain of loneliness again; until another soft cheek smiles and eases the way.

Leon is sixty-five. He still loves his wife, though she left him over a year ago. At first he filled empty nights with shapely shadows who drank away his money and laughed at his old-fashioned, fumbling passes. Now he finds them dull; he sits in half-darkness, fortified by television. His loneliness unleashes unmanly tears. Leon waits for a miracle —for someone to love.

Jim is lonely too. On Sunday mornings the paper gets blurry as he reads. A widower, Jim weeps for happy days past and those so empty now.

Well, now, that's enough. And not to make you cry, but laugh. Get out your diggers and start uncovering this dormant wealth of unloved males.

Go get 'em girl.

Maybe you won't find *all* the King's men, but it only takes one to win.

How about you who don't want deliverance by male? Okay for you, too. It's a brave new world with a new breed of women. But you *will* want Sam once in a while. It's kind of nice to hear a deep voice asking, "What's for supper?" And it's good for the girl to drag out *The National Observer* and just discuss it with a groovy male.

However, if you're hardy and staunch, your independence is a plus for weaker players. Every female we can scratch makes the going easier. Kind of puts the tally up *our* alley.

We'll take all you can't use. Or, if you'll pardon the slight, all those that can't use you.

One more how about. How about Greta? She has four little luvs all under ten. Where should, what should, how should . . .

Well, Greta, your problem is the greatest. You probably won't have the time to be as lonely as childless Mary, but the rest of the solo scene will be twice as hard. If you have money, a man isn't all that important. In this case you can hire the help. If you don't, you're undone. Children make divorce difficult.

For them the hurt goes on; for you there isn't much time to go.

You could move to a kibbutz, but maybe you can't.

It's tough. Being both Mama and Papa requires

the wisdom of Solomon and the patience of Job.

Meeting the next man in your life isn't easy anyway, but complications are tripled with children to think of.

There are some advantages in babysitting, however.

Strolling around the local zoo on a Sunday afternoon you might meet a papa with his weekend family taking in the monkeys. Toy sailboats in the park lake are fun for part-time fathers. Why not add a feminine flourish to your young'ns' playtime yawl. And while you're at it meet the senior sailors.

If you've got bambinos, you're likely to be young, and *that* is the bonus beyond compare. Don't despair. The kids can be a come-on and your youth and beauty the final touch.

The older, childless divorcée has other problems. Maybe yours will be solved more readily.

At first divorce brings more than separation from a man. Divorce disrupts a pattern. Links of a chain are shattered; lights flicker out; a way of life must be unlearned.

And lady, the division is usually rough. The peace you wrested from a stormy marriage isn't peace at all. Not at first.

Just loud silence. Empty minutes that make hours and days, sometimes months.

Then suddenly—serenity.

You've taken the plunge.

Now swim.

There's a prize on the opposite shore. For sure.

But you've got to move your arms and kick.

No life jackets, no floating logs. You've *got* to make it on your own. All around you others will be fighting to survive the same swim.

Once out of the woods and into the groove, nobody can bully you anymore. If you've done your homework, it won't be any problem to skip over hurdles and avoid hassles *whenever* they appear.

Get loose.

Expecting too much makes for disappointments by the carload. Expecting too little dims your view. Just believe that life has a little good and a little bad with a touch of passion and a sprinkling of delight for everybody (male or female).

It isn't Christmas all the time.

Really now, you can have a ball. Who knows what adventure waits each bright new morning as you set out for the office, what glamorous new man will suddenly appear to whisk you off to lunch? What praise and recognition will boost you up the company ladder?

Aim for the top. Keep your chin, chest, and shoulders high! Because you deserve the best!

Good looking, good loving, and most of all—good luck!